WHO AM I?

The true story of a woman who had been taken from her Mohawk Reservation as a baby and raised in a mentally and physically abusive home. Follow her personal journey toward finding her identity, native roots, family, and happiness.

Michelle Rice-Gauvreau

I dedicate this book to my adoptive father, Tom. The strongest Mohawk I ever knew. How I wish you could have lived to see me grow-up.

ACKNOWLEDGEMENTS

First and foremost, thank you to my husband, Michael, for always standing by me. Thank you, Raymond, my son, for loving me as your mom, quirks, and all. You both taught me about unconditional love. I love you both more than you could ever imagine.

Thank you to my birth mother, Sharon, for welcoming me back to the reservation. I'm so glad we were able to reconnect. I love you. Always.

To my foster parents, Elaine, and Geoff. You stood by and supported me during my most difficult teen years, and you still stand by me today. Thank you!

To my writing coach, Lisa Lelas. Thank you! You are not only my book coach but a true friend. I could never have done this without your endless support! I am forever indebted to you!

To all my adoptee friends, this book is for you! I hope it helps you find peace and strength in your journey.

LETTER TO MY READERS

Dear Fellow Adoptee,

I am thinking about you today. Thinking about how you are doing with your own adoption. I hope you are celebrating life, the good and bad moments, and your accomplishments. I would love to hear from you.

As an adoptee advocate, I hear from many adoptees who have struggled with their circumstances. I realize that some of us weren't as lucky as other adoptees. Many of us are happy and have no issues with their adoptions. Many of us have had reunions with our birth parents with both good and bad outcomes. I know there are no easy answers or fixes for us. We are our own unique beings.

Then, there are those like me who are adopted simply doing our best to get through each day. For us, there seems to be no easy path. I promise you that we will see light again many times over. Trust me, there is still so much to be grateful for.

As a Native American child, I have lived through an illegal adoption taking me from my Mohawk reservation roots in Canada to the States, eventually being raised by a mentally ill white woman. Personally, I couldn't comprehend my own circumstances. I knew I was different. Some of you have come to understand your adoption. I applaud all of you.

I remember the year I found out I was adopted. For years, I couldn't make sense of things and my coping skills were less than optimal. I had to go through a lot of therapy to learn how to heal. I didn't know how I would get through those times. I admit there are still days where I ask "why me?" Now I look at the life I have built and have found gratitude, peace and light. That is something I hope all adoptees find.

You are never alone, my friend. I am standing with you, holding your hand. Let me show you how to find your own peace and light as we walk through my journey together.

I love you all and there is absolutely nothing you can do about it.

Michelle

FORWARD…

I first met Michelle through her eBay Sellers Meetup Group. She had asked me, as a business coach, to come speak to her group about organizing and strategizing success in growing their businesses. After that presentation, I invited Michelle to be a guest on my cable-TV show to discuss life balance as a legal assistant, a successful eBay seller, wife, and mother. From the outside looking in, she certainly seemed to have it all.

I had no idea at that time that she only got into eBay selling to get rid of thousands of collectables her mother had left her with after she passed. She grew up the child of a hoarder, at a time none of us really knew what hoarding was or the depths of the mental illness behind it. Michelle was an only child and basically grew up without any close friends. No one could visit her home because hoarding had taken over the house. Even basic household necessities, such as a refrigerator, stove were non-existent and the toilet seldom worked.

Over the years, Michelle and I would keep in touch. I eventually learned of Michelle's Native American heritage. Born on a Mohawk reservation outside of Montreal, Canada, and for all intents and purposes, illegally adopted and taken as a baby to be raised by this white woman in Connecticut, suffering from mental illness. I suggested she share her fascinating back story to help bring awareness of the injustices within native communities but also to shed light on living in the shadow of mental illness. As a book-writing coach, I helped her get started and kept her on track page by page. It's time to share her story with the world.

Who Am I? is a moving and powerful memoir with just the right touch of human relatability, tenacity, and a touch of humor amidst a dark childhood endured by the author. The reader is transported to the 1960's and 1970's, at a time when mental illness was not discussed and safety measures not yet in place to protect loved ones in harm's way.

What Michelle Rice-Gauvreau experienced, after being taken from her native roots, spotlights an ever-growing problem in indigenous communities throughout the world, especially within our own native reservations here in North America. Trials with coping, understanding, and trying her best to forge a better life path without having any core sense of unconditional love, belonging or even family, is a true testament to her spirited DNA, she can only attribute to her Mohawk bloodline.

Michelle's captivating story is unfortunately one of thousands amongst indigenous people treated as outcasts and less than deserving. It is her hope that sharing her personal journey can shed some light on tragedies happening every day, still today, to native children who are taken, kidnapped, illegally adopted, and even murdered. Despite her heartbreaking circumstances, perhaps Michelle is one of the lucky ones.

-Lisa Lelas
Magazine Publisher, Writing Coach & Bestselling Author of
'*Simple Steps: 10 Weeks to Getting Control of Your Life*'
(Penguin/Random House, NY)
www.LisaLelas.com

TABLE OF CONTENTS

PREFACE

This is a true story about my 50 plus year journey being an adoptee.

I'm a Native American born on a Mohawk reservation in Canada but raised by a mentally ill white woman in Connecticut. I started writing this book on my birthday September 2 as a way of closure for myself. I decided it was time to share my adoption story. I realize now that instead of looking back at the constant turmoil and sadness, life actually gifted me with an incredible attitude, strength and vision to become the strong woman, wife and mother I am today. I hope to help others who struggle with their own adoption and encourage those thinking about adopting. Adoptions can be forever life changing. I feel firmly that it takes a village to help adoptees become happy and well-adjusted.

My adoption and my life growing up were not perfect. I think it may have looked acceptable to outsiders because I had to put on a good face to get through each day. I believe fate intervened because there were so many twists and turns in my journey, some of which caused me to fall, but somehow, I always stood back up and pushed forward. I believe fate has a plan for all of us.

This is where it all began...

There can be no keener revelation of a society's soul than the way in which it treats its children.

Nelson Mandela

CHAPTER 1 – MY BIRTH

September 1969

It was a hot and humid morning on the Kahnawake Indian Reserve (formerly spelled Caughnawaga) on the south shore just outside of Montreal on the banks of the St. Lawrence Seaway. Despite being a native reservation for hundreds of years, the reserve appears like any other Canadian or American suburb to an outside visitor but without street names. Modern homes mixed with original rustic stone houses made from rock and mud now hold families of the 21st century. This beautifully scenic suburban 'village' is clustered around an old Catholic Church, St. Francis Xavier built in 1720.

At this time, in the 1960s, there were about 2,500 Kahnawake Mohawk tribe members. Today, I believe there are more than 8,000 tribal members. They are stoic and independent people, yet still community and family oriented. They are proud people. People of the flint. Within the Confederacy, they were "keepers of the eastern door." Today, the reservation is a bustling town full of Mohawk nation members, small businesses, and a tight knit traditional community.

Early on Tuesday, September 2nd of 1969, a young and beautiful Kahnawake native of 20 years old went into

1

premature labor with her second born child- me. She was rushed to the hospital just outside of the reservation where she lived, with my feet apparently dangling out of her body while still in the car. I guess I was in a hurry. Breech birth. I was born only moments later, feet first, at 8:06 a.m. I can giggle about it now but ultimately; I know how dangerous a breech birth can be. Born about six weeks early, I was placed in a hospital nursery incubator for several days until I gained enough weight. If I had to guess the timeline, I was probably there for about eight days.

In the hours after my birth, Sharon told her hospital roommate, Gloria, that she was being forced by my grandmother to give me up for adoption. I am assuming that Gloria was also native from Kahnawake as well. Forcing Sharon to give me up for adoption was not meant to be cruel in any way. My grandmother, Mary, and her daughter, Sharon had a strained relationship off and on for many years. Financially it was not feasible to bring home another baby. My grandmother was raising my older brother, Mike. It was neither my grandmother's nor Sharon's choice to give me up. Reality had to sink in, and it was for the best; or so they thought at the time. I believe they both felt a tremendous loss for having to make this choice.

"Hello. I'm Gloria." Gloria would introduce herself.

"Hi," Sharon said shyly.

"Did you just have your baby this morning?" Gloria would ask looking at Sharon with concern.

"Yes," Sharon seemed very distraught.

"Is there anything I do for you?" Gloria really wanted to help Sharon.

"I have to give my daughter up and I don't want to." Sharon confessed.

"Oh no, I'm sorry Sharon." Gloria wanted to reach out and hug her but she herself was confined to bed for a couple of days.

"Do you have any plans for your baby?" Gloria asked consolingly, "How are you putting her up for adoption?"

2

"I don't know yet. Maybe the hospital will have an answer, or I may have to give her up to the Church." Sharon was very sad. Apparently, she did not want to give me up for adoption, but she didn't have a choice.

"I might have an answer for you Sharon. Let me make a couple of calls." Gloria smiled.

To help give Sharon an option while still in the hospital, Gloria called a friend of hers. This friend would become my adoptive father, Tom, who was also Native American, 52 years old, from the same reservation, but living in Connecticut. He was a 6 foot something, tall and handsome, rugged gentleman. He lived and loved life to the fullest. I had been told he left the reservation when he was 11 and basically raised himself in New York. He joined the U.S. Army and served in World War II; receiving a purple heart for his service on D-Day in Belgium after losing his leg to a land mine. He became an ironworker; most notably working on the Twin Towers in New York City.

Gloria proceeded to pick up and dial the phone to call someone to get Tom's phone number.

"Hi Ma?" She said.

"Do you have Tom's phone number? I need it, it's important." She was in a hurry. She wrote it down and hung up quickly. Gloria looked at Sharon, her eyes bright, and held up her index finger as if to tell Sharon not to go anywhere.

Gloria dialed the phone. Several rings must have felt like an eternity for Sharon but somebody picked up the phone on the other end.

"Halloo...?" Tom would answer in a jovial voice. This was his way of greeting all callers.

"Hey, Tom! It's Gloria! How are ya?" Gloria asked.

"Oh, hey Gloria, we're good...all is good. What's going on?" He asked, surprised at her call.

"Well, I think I have good news for you," Gloria practically sang.

"Really? What is it?" Tom seemed excited.

"Do you remember the family of Frank and Mary?" She asked.

"Yea, yea I do … why?" Tom was now wondering.

"Well, their daughter Sharon just gave birth to a baby girl. A little bit early, but Sharon is giving her up for adoption!" She was so excited and nearly out of breath.

Sharon was staring at Gloria in wonder with tears in her eyes. She knew she would have to say good-bye to me within days.

"Yes, we'll take her!" He didn't hesitate for one second. "I'll be there tomorrow."

They said their goodbyes and the planning began. Sharon was in tears and did not know what to say but got out of bed to walk down towards the nursery to gaze at me.

Tom was ecstatic and couldn't wait to come see me. He told Gloria that he would fly to Canada the next morning to start the 'process.' Coincidentally, he would later realize he worked with my birth grandparents years before. Tom knew so many people. Apparently, it is a small world on a native reservation where everyone knows everyone.

The next morning, Tom arrived in Kahnawake. He had charisma and seemed to charm his way into getting whatever he needed, and that charm led him to a lot of success in life. He began final preparations for the adoption procedure, probably knowing that what he was doing was not legal.

Since he knew a woman in Kahnawake named Henrietta who worked at the Mohawk membership department, he was able to forge some paperwork for the adoption process. Then he secured everything from a rental car to plane tickets from Montreal to Connecticut. They reserved time at the Catholic Church to have me baptized and began strategizing how best to create my birth certificate, which was nothing, but words written

4

on a single sheet of yellow-lined paper. Interestingly, this woman, Henrietta, who played the role as my Godmother, was someone I would never actually meet. Although I believe Tom had good intentions, this 'adoption' would cause me many problems later on in my life, much of which had to be legally rectified. In 1969 (and in the decades before I was born), apparently it was justified on reservations for many native babies to be given up for adoption or sent to Catholic residential schools. It's come to light only recently through the news media that so many native babies were kidnapped, lost or murdered through the system or a lack thereof. I always wondered what would have happened to me if I had actually been sent to an orphanage or a residential school. Would I have been lost in the system? Today's research show that over 50% of native children are either in foster care or adopted in Canada and so much is undocumented.

While I lay in the nursery incubator, Tom went back to the social services office in Kahnawake to falsely claim that he had a child with his wife in Connecticut and wanted me put on their membership roles. This is how the census was kept at that time. My given name on my birth/baptismal certificate is *Marie Lea Michelle Otisto Rice. (Otisto* in Mohawk means Star in English.) Michelle is what I have been called all my life.

The roles would entitle me to certain benefits on the land, such as owning a land plot to build a home, health benefits, burial benefits and education benefits- as long as I did not marry outside of the community. I would grow up very unaware that there were certain benefits as a Native American that I would lose if I married a white man.

Had things been done the right way, you could have considered my adoption as an "international adoption;" it wasn't a closed or open adoption. In reality, it was not an adoption at all, but rather an oral agreement between Tom and Sharon (and presumably my grandmother). There was no legal birth certificate, no adoption papers or agreements drawn up or signed.

Tom came to the hospital often to see me; anxiously awaiting to take me home with him. Being a very small, premature baby weighing 4lbs 7oz, it would be several days before that would happen.

Sharon, still clad in her hospital gown, would see Tom smiling as he gazed through the baby nursery window down the hospital corridor often taking polaroid photos of me. This gave her some comfort. The meetings that followed in the hospital were always very cordial. Tom made sure with Sharon that she was doing this willingly. She didn't feel she had a choice; she told him that she was. Sharon believed Tom was a hardworking, family-oriented gentleman, and that her daughter would be well taken care of.

After I was released from the neo-natal unit after being born prematurely, Sharon held me one last time. She put me in Tom's arms and proceeded to sign me out of the hospital. He turned to her and promised to send photos although I don't think that promise was ever kept. Tears in her eyes as she watched from her hospital room doorway as Tom walked away with her newborn daughter. She hoped she was doing the right thing...I believe she truly wanted nothing but the best for me. She went home to continue life as she knew it .... except now with a hole forever seared into her heart.

One of the last things to be done was to have me baptized in the local Catholic Church in Kahnawake with several people standing in witness. Henrietta stood in as my godmother and another woman stood in pretending to be Lea, his wife. I was never told who that was, but I am guessing it was a member of Tom's family.

The next morning, Tom carried me off in his rental car, headed to the airport. At that exact moment my native roots were ripped away from the Mohawk community.

My life would begin in the United States.

CHAPTER 2 – THE HOMECOMING

Mid-September 1969

By the time all was said and done, as far as the 'adoption' went, it was time to go 'home'. I was two weeks and two days old when I left the hospital and Kahnawake. Tom and I flew to Connecticut from Canada with me on his lap.

When the airplane landed and screeched to a halt at Bradley Airport, I arrived in Connecticut. It must have been such a sight in the 1960s to see a tall, handsome rugged-looking Native American man traveling solo with a newborn baby. I'm sure we received first-class treatment from the pretty stewardesses, and smiles from all the passengers alike.

As he strolled on into the terminal with me tightly in his arms, he went to baggage claim and winked at the airport employee standing nearby at a counter, asking her to watch me while he used the men's room. As the airport employee held me, there was yet another woman watching everything very closely. Lea.

Lea watched every move that was made with me. She was 44 years old at the time. She had come to the airport with a friend to pick us up. When Tom was out of sight, she quickly came over to the counter to claim me from the young employee and as she did, Tom was disappointed when he emerged from the restroom to see her holding me.

"Awww, I was hoping to surprise you!" he grunted.
"Too late!" She grunted back.

They kissed and looked at me sleeping in her arms.

From what I understand, Tom and Lea met in Brooklyn, New York, at a bar. Tom worked in the ironwork industry and Lea had the jobs of a cook and waitress. Together, they had an intense relationship. I heard different stories that there was a lot of alcohol involved in some of those intense moments.

They were married in December 1958, in Kahnawake, having been together for three years before that. This would be Tom's second marriage but Lea's first (that I knew of at the time). They tried to have children of their own, but it would not be in the cards. So, it was eleven long years before I came along.

While the Catholic Church recognized their marriage in Kahnawake, it seemed that the Mohawk community did not accept mixed marriages well, even though it was more common than not. This would be part of the reason that Lea did not come to Canada with Tom to 'adopt' me. While it was an odd situation, Lea stayed behind to get the house ready.

They took me home from the airport and placed me in a white, wrought-iron cradle that Lea bought for my arrival. Looking at old photographs, it seemed as if I lived in a rich home with all the fancy décor in those pictures. Tom would call it "Lea's Big Rich Home" as it was written on the back of an old photograph. As an infant, I would sleep in their bedroom until I was at least two years old. Funny story, I guess I would 'interrupt' Mommy and Daddy time and that's when they decided to put me in my own room.

Obviously, I have no clear memory of the first three years of my life, but I am told there were family gatherings to welcome me both in Connecticut and in Rhode Island where extended family resided. I'm told that both Tom and Lea loved me very much. Time would tell. I do believe that both Tom's and Lea's families adored me. Crazily though, I would not have much contact with people in either family, except for maybe a few relatives on Lea's side.

I would start to grow up and I knew that Tom loved me. He was my Daddy for all intents and purposes. He really did devote himself to me as my father. In old photographs you can see his love unequivocally. I am sad to have not known him anymore than time would let me.

As time went on, I would hear great stories about him from people in Connecticut and from others in Kahnawake. I never met his family members in Kahnawake even when I eventually went to meet my birth family in my teen years. As for others who knew him, he was affectionately known as Peg-Leg because of his wooden leg he had a result of stepping on a landmine in Belgium during World War II. He was a war hero and received a Purple Heart for his bravery and service in the Army.

I am sure my needs were met as Tom saw to that while he was alive. I'm sure I was more than spoiled with Daddy. I believe he loved me. He worked hard for his family over the next three years, and he never wavered. He had plans that he handwrote to start a big garbage removal business in Connecticut and in Canada. He had plans to make sure I was given a good life, that both Lea and I wanted for nothing, and to make sure I knew my birth family. So many plans with so little time as his life was suddenly cut short. He was diagnosed with metastatic lung cancer at the Veterans Administration Hospital in Connecticut and died on July 27, 1972, peacefully at home, within five months of his diagnosis. This seemed to be very sudden and it came as a shock to Lea and I think the entire family, both his and hers.

My life changed the moment he died.

CHAPTER 3 – SUDDEN DEATH

July 1972

I was nearly three years old when Tom died in July 1972. According to his death certificate, the cause of death was metastatic lung carcinoma.

Tom received treatment for his cancer after his diagnosis, which ultimately rendered him disabled in the last months of his life. Lea never told me how Tom felt about his diagnosis or whether he was hopeful that he would beat the cancer. During his career in both the army and as an ironworker, he was exposed to a lot of asbestos as well as smoking cigarettes, and obviously these were part of the cause as well.

Tom died suddenly in the middle of the night. Lea would tell me later while she was not in the bedroom at the moment he died, she heard him take a long deep breath as he passed. She knew he was dead. It was a surprise to her. She called the neighbors and her sister for support. Lea called the authorities to come and pronounce him and the funeral home came to take his body. It was just one gentleman who placed Tom's tall body in a body bag onto the gurney and wheeled him to the hearse. I was asleep through it all.

After my father's death, many visitors apparently came to console my mother. I have just a few faded memories. I remember bits and pieces of his funeral.

11

These were my first real memories. Kind of weird being almost three years old.

On the day of the funeral, it was a bright sunny day and I remember a large crowd and the wooden coffin. What I don't remember is the funeral mass at the local Catholic Church. I remember the cemetery where I was taken across the pathway to a headstone with a statue to be distracted. I remember the gun salute scared me. Tom was buried with full military honors. I remember the flag being given to Lea, which I found years later hidden under a sofa and is now in a shadow box along with his army tags displayed proudly on my bookshelves.

Once the funeral was over, family and friends came back to the house. Unfortunately, Lea thought that by not having a gathering afterwards, that would make people leave sooner. She didn't want anyone around. That didn't happen. People came back to the house anyway. Tom's sister Alline would send her husband out to the local store to get coffee and lunchmeats for everyone. Lea was less than pleased. I think she hated his family. She didn't want them around-whether for my sake or hers, I don't know.

People left a few days afterwards. Lea cut off all contact with everyone on my father's side, not realizing that much of the truth would come back to haunt her years later. That cutoff included Tom's mother Annabelle in Kahnawake, who was beside herself when Tom passed away. But the cutoff would only happen after Lea took care of certain business matters regarding his will.

Lea went after everything that was financially owed to her. Tom's will stipulated that everything he owned would go to Lea and if she had died, everything would go only to me despite having other children in prior relationships. I wonder if Lea had any influence over that.

After Tom's death, Lea went to Kahnawake, but she did not go alone. Her sister had come along for the ride and to keep me hidden while Lea was taking care of business. She had to settle the property issues there since she was not allowed to keep it being a white woman.

She was advised to keep the land for me if I chose to go back and build a house one day, but she absolutely refused and sold it back either to the reservation or to Tom's mother, Annabell. Learning this after I became an adult made me kind of angry that she wouldn't keep the land for me, but after many years, I think I understand why…maybe.

Over the next several months after that, Lea went to the local hospitals in NY and CT looking for answers as to how and why my father died after only being diagnosed with lung cancer five months before. Not sure what she was looking for there, but one could surmise that she may have been looking to see if he knew he was sick for longer than he let on, or even for someone to blame for his illness and ultimately his death. I don't know if she ever found the answers she was looking for but she knew she had to move on if only for both of our sakes.

I think Tom's death took a piece of both of us with him, although I did not know it at the time. Something would always be missing and there were so many questions that went unanswered.

So began my life without Daddy.

Michelle Rice Gauvreau

CHAPTER 4 – TURBULENT LIFE WITH LEA

July, 1972 – April, 1984

I'm not even sure where to begin. How do I explain my childhood and early teen years? They all seem so vividly blurry. Explaining how I grew up will be no easy task. Growing up was less than ideal with some good moments and many bad moments.

Just months after my father's death, Lea moved us to new home on the other side of town. While it was a nice house on the outside set back surrounded by woods and a reservoir, inside it was anything but idyllic. I never had my own space. I would sleep on a fold-up cot somewhere amongst cardboard boxes everywhere.

I remember Lea enrolled me in nursery school but most of those memories are a blur. I remember eating oatmeal raisin cookies, playing on the playground, and swinging on the swings. I also remember clearly being scared of other parents so much so that I would hide in a corner when a parent came into the classroom. I didn't realize it at the time but after Tom died Lea kept both of us isolated from the world.

Kindergarten came and I went to a school just up the road from our house. I remember nap times and my teacher. The only clear memory I have is of some of the neighborhood kids and the class photo we had, although I had no friends.

I could never make friends within my class or the neighborhood kids because of Lea. She never let me have friends

15

over nor could I go over to their homes. Our house was always so cluttered. I wasn't aware of what hoarding was at the time. Because of my isolation, I was considered weird or worse by other children. I was bullied and harassed quite a bit growing up in that neighborhood. Throughout my childhood, I had no idea that I was adopted. For some reason, several neighborhood kids believed I was adopted and would taunt me with it, but I ignored them thinking they were just lying to upset me. I felt like what they were saying had some truth to it but left it alone. It is amazing to think that rumors about my adoption were swirling around the neighborhood, but I chose to trust my mother. Lea vehemently denied everything, and I believed her.

Lea became very depressed, and her mental health began declining. As a child, I had no idea. Growing up with a woman who undoubtedly was depressed was tough for me. She was angry and volatile. I often cried myself to sleep at night. She was not well but I was unaware. Her family was rarely involved with us other than the occasional holiday or family get together at other relatives' houses. I didn't dare tell anyone about my life at home. We had no support from friends or family. Most of the time, Lea would keep them at bay.

Even at home, Lea never let anyone in. On a rare occasion, her sister, Shirley, would come over or perhaps a plumber or electrician. That was it. There seemed to be no real family connection from any direction. She would not keep the house clean. Lea's depression morphed into a classic hoarding situation. We never had a stove or fridge. She kept a hotplate on top of an old dresser in the so-called kitchen. She kept milk and anything else she bought cold in Styrofoam coolers. The house became a nightmare. The furniture never dusted, the rugs never vacuumed, the bathroom toilet was to be flushed only once a week and was never cleaned or sanitized. Any dresser or closet was utilized by her and her only. My clothes were kept in boxes. I was not allowed to touch or move anything. We had insects and critters all through the house. Mold was growing and made me sick at times. There were holes in the walls with exposed wiring and cobwebs everywhere. Everything was stuffed dust and rodent nesting. The creepy cement basement would flood every time it rained ruining the many hoarded boxes she had on the floor, time and time again. It was nothing but mold and mud.

There were winters where she could not even afford to put the heat on. We never had air conditioning in the summer, as the house, according to her, was cool enough. This was something Tom would have never allowed if he were still alive at the time. I know he would have made sure I had everything I needed as I was told the same by many people.

We had a large plot of land, nearly two acres, that seemed to overgrow as the years went on. Lea mowed the front lawn sometimes, but the backyard was not as kept up. Occasionally, she would hire a man with a tractor to mow everything except the wild garden that was there. There was an acre of tall pine trees that she would sell for Christmas trees, but in time they grew way too tall to be sold. I remember there was a strawberry patch, a row of blueberry and current bushes, some raspberries, and vines of grapes. Over the years they would disappear. I used to love to pick fruit because we barely had anything fresh to eat in the house.

During those first five years after Tom's death, it seemed that is all we did in the summers was walk the narrow pathway to the vegetation to gather our food. As a little girl, I have these few memories of having fun with Lea in the backyard. She would point out little critters and I found it fascinating to play in the dirt and chase the bunnies and field mice around.

I would listen to and watch the hawks and other large birds circle above or sit in the tall trees as they hunted their prey. I would watch the bees and butterflies do what they do. I would look out for our cat, Heather, who would follow Lea like a puppy all over the yard. I would watch the water ripple on the reservoir next door and see the fish swim in the beautiful clear water. Sometimes I would see other people sitting, swimming, or fishing by the water behind our property. Those first few years were actually good years with my mother until I got older. I didn't understand mental illness, hoarding or isolation.

17

There was a dark side to Lea. That dark side was full of abuse, rage, depression and talked to herself often. She never sought help for herself and made sure to blame me for her troubles. She would tell me that I was the one who needed the help. She was not eligible for any assistance, and I often watched her struggle financially and mentally. Lea often called me a burden. We would live hand to mouth most of the time. That would become so evident as I got older. But there was also a side to her that would be giving at times. Sometimes I would wake up in the morning and find books that she would give me to read. I enjoyed reading.

From the 1960s through the 1980s, Lea owned apartments in which she was labeled a "slumlord." She rented to students and low-income people. Oftentimes when things needed repair, she was never able to get them fixed for long periods of time due to financial struggles. My father, Tom, had originally invested in these apartments. It was a shame that Lea let them go to shambles. She was lucky if she was paid the rent owed to her each month from the tenants she had. The apartments were near a university, so most of her tenants were struggling students and young families. The apartments were destroyed many times over and she had to repaint, replace appliances, and have repairs done over and over again. I remember having to be with her while this was all going on. She would work in the places mostly on weekends. I would get to know the tenants, their kids, and pets. I sometimes made friends with the kids that moved in but that never lasted long because they would move or were evicted. Some of the tenants were nice and often offered me treats or gifts, much to Lea's disgust at times. I particularly remember one tenant, an older lady, who told me how much she loved me every time that she saw me. I rarely heard that from my own mother. It always felt nice to hear those words from that lady, but I watched Lea grind her teeth. All that aside, I understood that this was her primary way of supporting us.

Lea was an introvert at best. She went out only when she had to. If she went to a grocery store, she would buy the cans with no labels in the clearance carts in the back of the store. She would go to tag sales, rummage sales, flea markets where I would get most of my clothes. She didn't know how to manage finances and she never trusted banks. When she did have a few dollars, she would buy "collectibles" and just stack them up wherever she could find space in the house.

As I grew older, I began asking questions about our lifestyle and why we had to live this way. Hoarders tend to become defensive when they are asked questions.

As she became more and more frustrated with me, it was evident that she just didn't want me anymore. As a child, I never felt her love. Lea would look for people to take me in. Her sister, Shirley, took me in for a few days, but when Lea saw my happiness with my aunt, she brought me back home, perhaps feeling a bit jealous. I don't think Lea ever believed I deserved happiness. By the time I was around 13 years old, Lea "couldn't handle me" anymore. She would tell anyone who would listen that I was "awful and undeserving." She asked people to take me in. Most people assumed she was kidding. She wasn't. She even went so far as to find out information to legally emancipate me, or to have me married at a very young age. She had no luck with either of those scenarios.

Lea put on a good act when she had to. There was lots of fighting, both physical and verbal, with her behind closed doors. I became an angry child seemingly desperate for a parent's love. I obviously had a lot of issues to work out and Lea did not help. No matter what, her finger was pointed at me telling me everything was always my fault.

While she never worked an actual job, she found ways to make money aside from the apartments she owned. She became an Avon representative, but mostly bought Avon products to store in the house, which became part of the hoard. She would also set up at flea markets with stuff that she bought at tag sales and thrift stores. On good days at the flea market, she would make some decent money. Between her weekend flea market sales, the apartment building income and Tom's social security benefits, we should have been able to live comfortably but Lea somehow foolishly spent the money.

What I didn't know at the time was why she was being referred to as a slumlord. There were many newspaper articles written in the town newspaper about her non-compliance with paying taxes and repairs going unattended. I remember a teacher in public middle school showing me an article about the local Town Hall meeting that took place to condemn the apartments she owned. Lea would ultimately agree to make the necessary repairs but would never actually complete them. I started to understand.

Lea would sometimes trust some of the tenants to keep her informed of the "goings-on" at the property. There was one tenant, Tex, who decided to do more than just keep an eye on the place or make repairs. He would tell personal stories to Lea about how he used to beat and abuse his children when they were younger to keep them 'in line'. Lea was more intrigued about keeping me 'in line' and how she could do that. She began relying on his parental advice. I think she thought he would be the end-all be-all answer to her prayers, and I would straighten out immediately. Well, he was more than happy to offer his solution by giving her a thick leather strap to hit me with when things were out of hand at home. If I uttered one wrong thing or argued with Lea, I would absolutely get that beating from her. She would chase me with that strap, and it didn't matter where she hit me with it. I got it in the head, face, and arms more than anything because I tried to defend myself. I still get angry when I think about that today. How dare she!

This is why I vowed as I became an adult that I would NEVER raise my children in such a manner.

The holidays with Lea were never joyous, really. Thanksgiving holidays came and went. As for the Christmas holidays, she loved to go holiday shopping because in her words, she "loved the atmosphere." She bought things for herself and just left them in boxes around the house to collect dust. A hoarder's paradise. She was never truly in the holiday spirit. It would be a rare Christmas if I received a gift that I actually wanted, and it would be an even more rare Christmas if I gave her a gift with whatever allowance I saved. Any gift to Lea would be scoffed at and put aside.

Decorating the house was never something that she wanted. I begged for it because I used to love seeing the decorations in Church and she relented only on Christmas Eve. I remember a tiny white/pink Christmas tree that she placed by the back door of the house right next to the cat's litter box. A few years later, she would make a space in the already filled living room when she pulled out a large vintage silver tinsel tree she purchased at an auction and let me decorate it with vintage glass ornaments only to be put away the next day. The holiday was never truly enjoyed. She would also make sure to take me to "see Santa" and get a picture with him just to make things look good when we had to go to a family holiday dinner. We usually went to Aunt Shirley's and Uncle Bill's house for Thanksgiving and Christmas where things were a bit more cheerful. I was able to at least sit with my uncle, have snacks and watch TV with him. He was incredibly sweet to me.

Lea and I never took any real trips anywhere except to family reunions in Rhode Island every summer and maybe a trip to Massachusetts, but that would be all. Those particular trips stopped after a few years and I don't know why.

As for any real trips I would read and fantasize about, Lea would always tell me we would go somewhere someday. I would make a list of places I would have loved to have gone to, especially a place like Disney. It just never happened, and I never understood it.

In the summers, if I wasn't grounded or in some sort of trouble, she would take me to a place called Valley Falls Park near the house. It was the one place where she would enjoy reading the daily newspaper, have a cup of coffee and just be in her car with the doors open while I went to swim with the other kids and played games with the lifeguards in the pond for a couple of hours in the late afternoons. I loved swimming there.

Although there were a few moments of peace, it wasn't easy to swallow my life of hell living with Lea, but the truth would soon come out and it would rock my world further into an oblivion that I wasn't sure I would survive.

My School Years

Catholic School (a Polish Catholic School). Good ol' Saint Joseph's. I was such a misfit in school-private or public. That was until my last two years of high school.

From first through sixth grade, it was never a good time in Catholic school. It seemed like everything was a sin. There was a lot of bullying from both the kids and the teachers, not to mention some of the nuns including the principal. My third-grade teacher /nun decided to corner me in the coat closet to tell me I was not a child of God because I was "Indian" and adopted. What was she talking about? I was never sure how to ever talk to these nuns. I was intimidated by the mere sight of them and every time I told Lea what they did or didn't do or say, she would tell me I deserved it but made sure to tell me that my third-grade teacher lied to me about being adopted. Why would a nun lie to her students? It didn't seem okay to me. I used to think it was just the 'Catholic' way of doing things. I began to resent Catholic school.

I do remember in second grade that I was severely injured one day. We were at recess and some of us were playing tag and as hard as I was running, I remember tripping and everything went black for a few minutes. I finally came to and felt that I was getting carried down the stairs into the school cafeteria where I was placed in a chair in the cafeteria kitchen with the overpowering smell of cabbage and pierogis sending me into nausea. Blood was pouring down my face and I scraped both knees. Ouch! I remember the teachers and nuns all over me with kitchen rags and towels trying to stop the bleeding. I saw Father Al rushing in with his adorable little black Pomeranian, Missy, barking at anyone who came near me. Missy tried her hardest to soothe me by licking my blood-stained knees. Sweet little pup she was. Everyone seemed concerned. Lea had been called, and she rushed to the school. Everyone told her I needed to go to the hospital and get stitches in my head. She agreed to take me although she was unhappy about it; probably more out of concern for her wallet than for me really.

We arrived at the hospital and all I remember is getting stitches in my forehead and being told I need to stay in bed and not move my head too much. At the time, I wasn't sure why, but later on, Lea would tell me that I had a concussion as well. I don't remember too much from there. The small scar on my forehead, still visible just at the edge of my hairline, sometimes reminds me of that day, still feeling that phantom pain today.

Third and fourth grades seemed to be such a blur. However, when I got to fifth grade, I had the worst male teacher in all Catholic school, Mr. M. He loved to pick on the more vulnerable students, especially me, as a slightly chubby kid. Some days he would come up behind me and blow out his cheeks and stretch out his arms to make fun of my weight. I remember he didn't like me very much, and the feeling was mutual, but I was always respectful toward him. I was good at most of my subjects throughout that year, although he chose to not give me good grades, despite getting A's in other grades, he gave me C's. Lea would question my schoolwork when she received my report card and continued to berate me instead of seeking help or asking Mr. M why. I remember I began hating myself especially when looking in the mirror.

One day, it was stiflingly hot in his classroom, and I was not well. So not well in fact, that I tried to run out of class but before I could, I vomited right on his floor by the chalkboard while he was writing our homework. I was sent to the principal's office so I could sit. There was no nurse on duty so I went home at the normal time when school was dismissed because the school could not get a hold of Lea, or she just wouldn't answer the phone. I remember feeling so sick on the bus ride home that when I got off the bus crying, not able to walk all the way to my house, I walked slowly to the nearest house I could get to so I could call Lea. The people were nice enough to let me use the phone as I stood ill, sobbing uncontrollably at their doorway. They were kind enough to let me in.

Ring. Ring. Ring.

"Hello," Lea finally picked up the phone.

"Mommy...." I cried hysterically.

"I'm at the bus stop, I don't feel good, and I threw up at school and on the sidewalk. Please come get me?" I begged.

"No, I can't. You can walk home. It's not far." She was apparently waiting for her Avon Manager to come to the house. The Avon Manager obviously trumped her own daughter.

I cried as I left that neighbor's house to walk home, sobbing all the way.

By the time I got home I was out of breath. Weeping in pain and nausea, I knocked on the door loudly, yelling for her to please help me. I had to sit down on the cement step and lean against the door. Lea finally came to the door with a look on her face like she was going to kill me for interrupting her day.

"Get in here and go to your room, just lie down!" She hissed.

"Mom, I think I need to go to the doctor!"

"We'll see after the lady comes by." She really did not want to bring me anywhere for medical attention. She sent me to my room and told me to lie down and wait.

The Avon woman got there but was concerned for me as she heard me crying. I just couldn't help myself. I felt awful. The nice woman told Lea to take care of me and she would come back another time. Lea refused as she said she didn't think I was really sick. Ok. At that moment, I had to run into the nasty bathroom and vomit again, this time in the sink because the toilet was not working. The poor lady must have heard my vomiting and took that as a hint to leave.

24

After that, Lea finally decided to take me to an emergency room where they in fact told her I had the flu and I needed to rest for at least a week. She had nothing to say. I think she was very embarrassed and probably upset that she would have to pay for the medical care and medication. We had no health insurance. All I knew was I wanted to be in bed.

While I was sick, the one thing I hated was her cigarette smoke. I begged her not to smoke for the ride home from the hospital but of course, my pleas fell on deaf ears. At home, the cigarettes were worse. I'll never forget this. I think my whole body was reeling from the smell. However, I was home for a week and during this week, Lea seemed to be a little more generous toward me, giving me cool cloths on my head for my fever, giving me Campbell's alphabet soup if I felt like eating and even hugged me in her lap while we watched something on TV one night. This was foreign to me, but it felt good. She never left me alone that week. That was one of the few times in my life that I ever felt her genuine care.

By the time I returned to school a week later, I don't think Mr. M was fond of me for creating havoc that day I became sick, but to my pleasant surprise he never really bothered me again. He was even a little kinder to me. I think he was more than happy to let me move on to the next grade. He was certainly a piece of work and I always wondered years later what had happened to him.

The Suspicious "Break In" at Home

Not too long after being sick, another incident happened while in fifth grade was the time I finally was allowed to have my very own key to Lea's house. Before that, I would have to wait outside of the house alone if Lea wasn't home when I got off the bus. At times, if it was bad weather, I would go to a neighbor's house where they told me I was old enough to have a key to my own house. The same neighbors would often tell Lea that it was time for me to have said key. She always said she would think about it and leave it at that, frustrating our neighbors more. The last time I had to go to the neighbor's

25

house, it was the last straw for the neighbor, and that was when I finally received a key. Lea finally gave in. This would not go without incident, naturally.

The very first day I had my own key, trouble followed. I had come home to find the house in even more shambles than it had been before. I attempted to open the side door to the kitchen which seemed to be somewhat blocked by stuff. Once I finally pushed the door open, I sort of gasped. I noticed the back door open, and the bottom window was carefully taken out, panes and all. It appeared as if the house was broken into.

Several knick-knacks were knocked over, dresser drawers were pulled out and the contents were strewn about. I was scared and I called the police.

"Police Department, what is your emergency?" the dispatcher asked calmly.
"I think our house was broken into!" I tried not to be upset, but that failed.
"Ok, honey, what is your address? She asked.
I gave her our address.
"We'll be right there." She confirmed.
I waited for the officers. I heard a loud knock. Several officers and a detective were standing out front.
"Hi Michelle…what happened?" the Officer asked me nicely.
"Our house was broken into" I replied crying, tears streaming down my face.
"Ok, can we come in and look around?" He asked.

I nodded my head yes and was told to sit on the chair in the kitchen while they checked things out. They went through the house and asked me how I would know if it was a break-in since the house was in such disarray. I explained that the house was more of a mess than usual and one of the four-paned glass windows in the back door looked like it was taken out and the door was ajar. The officers looked at that. They seemed suspicious at that point and didn't try to investigate for fingerprints.

26

Another officer looked at a note my mother had left me about "cookies in orange", he asked me to explain what orange meant and I pointed to the Styrofoam cooler where it had my Hi-C drink in it. We never had a refrigerator. He looked and nodded as if he understood this.

"Is there someone you can call to come be with you?" I mentioned my Aunt Shirley. I was told to call her and did so crying.

I dialed the phone number and waited anxiously as it began ringing on the other end. My Uncle Bill picked up as I was crying pretty hard. He could barely understand me and got my aunt on the phone.

"Michelle, what's going on?" she asked, concerned.
"The house was broken into. Can you come here? The police would like you to come here." I asked, scared.
"I'll be right there." She hung up the phone. There was no hesitation.
It would be almost 20 minutes before I saw her car coming down the street, but I felt so much relief seeing her. The officer would have stayed with me but felt it better if I had family there too. He spoke with my aunt first and then left.

Because of the hoarding condition inside, my aunt chose to sit in her car with me.

I wanted to stay outside anyway but wasn't comfortable just sitting in the car. I just wanted to watch for Lea.

Finally, after what seemed like an eternity, I saw her burnt orange Dodge van coming down the street. She pulled in looking surprised to see her sister and myself outside. Before she could stop and turn the van off, I opened her driver's side door. My heart was pounding.

"Mom, I had to call the police!" I cried.
"WHAT?! Why would you do that?" She was flabbergasted as she got out of her car to go speak to her sister before rushing into the house.

"What happened?" she asked Aunt Shirley.

"According to the police, it seems as if your house was broken into from the back" she replied.

"Oh my God! Oh my God!" Lea rushed into the house screaming, running from room to room and then up into the attic like a maniac.

"Lea, do you want to get out and just get a coffee and a bite to eat?" my aunt asked, trying to get her to calm down. It seemed as if my aunt was suspicious that Lea was up to something. Funny, the cat we had didn't seem phased by anything and she was not acting scared as she came in through the back door looking to be fed.

We left to go down to the restaurant and it was awkward silence for a little while. We could tell Lea did not want to talk to either of us about anything. I was just glad Aunt Shirley was with us.

Aunt Shirley finally broke the silence by talking to her sister.

"Lea, what do you think was stolen?" she asked straightforwardly.

"I don't know yet!" Lea snapped at her sister. She did not want to talk about this in front of me. She never wanted to talk in front of me. Her attitude was that it was never any of my business.

Once we were done at the restaurant, Lea decided she did not want to go to the police station that night and said she would deal with it in the morning. This baffled us as she was supposed to go and sign the police report. I believe she was thinking about what to tell them because as it turned out, she had been at the dog races about an hour away, gambling with a cousin. How do you tell the police you left your daughter to fend for herself while you were out gambling? Today, that probably would have been negligence.

I learned later on from Aunt Shirley that the police returned to the house while I was at school the next day. They had suspected that Lea had broken into her own home. They questioned her if she was trying to make a claim for insurance money. She admitted she had no homeowner's insurance and never did. She refused to answer any more of their questions saying she was now nervous to go out and indicated that there had been strange cars and vans parked near the house. So, any vehicle parked near the house, her regular comment to me was, "I can't go out, they're watching us."

To be honest, I think Lea was trying to set me up for the "break-in," but she realized I was smarter than she gave me credit for. I think Aunt Shirley even knew what Lea was trying to do to me.

Life in Catholic school became more and more difficult for me. Sixth grade was a real eye opener with Sister S. We were told when to answer any questions and if the answer was wrong, she would literally push us by our shoulders back into our seats or punch us on our arms or buttocks. That made me just as fearful as being at home, and I could not take any more of this Catholic school. I begged Lea to go to public school; making the argument that it would not cost Lea anything as I knew she was not making tuition payments. I later confirmed this while cleaning out the house, finding a lot of old paperwork with the school threatening to sue her for the back tuition she owed.

While in Catholic school, there seemed to be lots of concern for me by the principal, priest and one other teacher. That one teacher, Mrs. W, was concerned that I did not have enough regular clothes and since she had an older daughter who was my size, she gave me some clothes. It was a generous gift, and I was thrilled to be able to dress somewhat decently outside of the school uniform. Lea, on the other hand, was not so thrilled. She seemed to give Mrs. W. glaring looks whenever a school function was in progress. I figured that she was just jealous or upset that another family was treating me nicely.

There was no doubt that Lea was not the most nurturing of parents. However, she never questioned the teachers and would go right along with them; especially if it included taking away any recess activities and/or any other punishment at school or at home.

Over the years, the Catholic school newsletter would be given to us each month with the parents' name handwritten on each. Lea would yell at me for writing on it. I told her the truth that it came that way, she would never believe me, and the yelling turned into being hit or sent to bed. Her name was written in cursive. I didn't know how to write in cursive at the time. I finally had to ask my teacher not to give me the school newsletter. I was facing enough fear at home. Sure enough, more psychological and physical abuse would come in different manners for years to come.

I may have been young, but I was at the end of my rope with both Lea and the Catholic school system. At the end of sixth grade, I begged Lea again to let me go to public school; giving her the idea that it could benefit her financially and that I may do better in school. She finally agreed. How clever was I?

My cleverness worked for a short while. I enrolled in the local middle school. Unfortunately, things became worse in the 7th and 8th grades. I continued having trouble in school because of the problems I was enduring at home. I didn't know it at the time, but I was becoming depressed and angry. I just did not want to deal with anything.

The bullying became worse in public school and things at home were not any better with Lea, just adding to my frustrations as she mocked me and told me I deserved whatever I got. There was no protection for her "daughter." I was broken in so many ways. I used to go to my guidance counselor's office a lot just because I felt safer there. I finally opened up about our problems at home, in tears, and he immediately put me in touch with the school's social worker, Mrs. M.

Mrs. M had reviewed my file and called Lea to discuss my progress at school and wanted to sit down with both of us. That was another day I dreaded going home. From the moment

I got home that day Mrs. M. called her, Lea unlocked the door as I never received my key back from the alleged "break in" a year or so before. She had a stern look on her face.

"Your social worker called me. You're doing poorly in school!" She screamed at me.

"You need to fix this problem. I don't have time to come in for a meeting but I'm being forced to for your stupidity," she hissed. In reality, she didn't want to miss her soap operas.

I didn't hear the end of things for at least a week. Once we finally met with the social worker at school, Mrs. M wanted to know more about home life. Lea had warned me prior to this meeting that I better not talk about her business or the house. I felt sick and trapped.

Mrs. M. could tell more was going on. She called for monthly school progress meetings with Lea, put me in touch with a tutor, and thought it would be beneficial to me to play some sort of sport like girls' softball. So, I signed up to play for a couple of years. I really loved that outlet, and I became a very good softball player. As for the monthly school progress meetings, I would not be allowed in as the school felt it would be better to speak to Lea alone. Naturally, that did not go so well as they had a difficult time getting Lea to participate. Mostly she would just fall asleep, and my teachers would have to wake her up. They were frustrated with her.

Eighth grade was not easy either but somehow it seemed a little better that year. It was a bit quieter in school and I involved myself in more activities. While the progress meetings still took place, I would stay after school to watch games in the gymnasium, or I would practice catching the softball with other players on our town teams. This is what I think made me a strong player and ultimately a great catcher, winning several games for the team. Those foul balls that were struck could never get past me.

The school added a great field trip to Boston where we went to the children's museum for a show and then to the Boston

Aquarium where I think I just wanted to stay. The best part was that the school social worker, Mrs. M, accompanied us as a chaperone. She really enjoyed all of us but she could be tough too making sure we as students behaved on a trip like this. I felt safe with her on that field trip and in school. I had no idea what was around the corner for me...

My high school years would be the most turbulent years of my life.

CHAPTER 5 – THE TRUTH SETS YOU FREE

I never skipped school until I got to high school. It was mostly peer pressure to look cool but really, I looked like an idiot and that was just during my first two years of high school. My clothes were not the latest fashion, and I was just another misfit amongst other misfits.

In my freshman year, I met my first high school boyfriend Tony. He was a senior. Not a very popular guy but nice. When I finally admitted, I didn't want to date him, he got angry and told me he would have been the best boyfriend ever. I had no interest plus I felt somewhat awkward being around him as I thought I would be judged for being with an older student. Ironically, I thought my heart was already with somebody outside of school so my relationship with Tony was short lived but we remained friends until I left town. My infatuation with this other guy Dave was beyond my control. I met him through my school friend Kimberly, the summer before high school. Kimberly was a classmate I had known since middle school. I often hung out with her after school and even went camping with her and her sister one weekend. During that camping trip I met Dave.

I was just shy of 15 when I met him. It was the summer of 1983, just before high school started. Kimberly and her sister invited me to go camping with them and a few other friends from their father's bowling league. I was surprised that Lea gave me permission to go. It had just rained, so it was muddy when we drove down the wooded trail to our campsite. As we were pulling the tent, food, and beer out of the car, I noticed a man setting up his tent near ours. Kimberly's sister introduced us, and he immediately seemed to have taken a liking to both Kimberly and me. He was a member of their bowling league, 32 years old, divorced, and the father of 2 young kids. He hung around with us at the pool, drinking beer, winking, and smiling throughout the day. He gave us a few beers. I choked the beer down trying not to let on that it was the very first time I ever drank alcohol. Surprisingly the beers went down easier the more I drank. I felt drawn to him for some reason. The rest of the evening was a blur. Kimberly told me the next day that I had to be helped to the showers because I had fallen in the mud. Regardless, I was experiencing my first hangover that morning.

Dave gave me his telephone number and told me to call him anytime. He was told by someone that I had a very strict mother, so he didn't want to call me. School resumed shortly after that weekend, and I realized I was a bit smitten with him.

Dave started pursuing me more through Kimberly telling her to have me call him on their bowling nights. She delivered the message the next day but seemed jealous. I began calling him from a payphone at school and he would pick me up occasionally after school. We would drive around town, and he would make moves on me as best as he could, always wanting me to do things I wasn't ready for at the time. I relented one ill-fated night in October, 1984.

Lea and I had gotten into another one of our regular blowouts where she was throwing dishes and whatever else she could at me. With my arms covering my face, I ran out of the house and down the road in the dark. I called Dave begging him to come get me. He found me hiding behind a restaurant down the street and drove me to a dark parking lot. He took advantage of my vulnerability that night. I lost my innocence. It was an emotional night for me having just been in a fight with Lea and running to Dave to save me. I thought Dave's kind of back-seat love was real love. In my young mind, I thought we would be together 'forever' since I had given myself to him. I would later learn the truth that sex and love were two very different dynamics.

Dave had to bring me back to Lea's but dropped me off away from the house, so she didn't see him. I didn't want to go home but knew I had no choice. As I got to the door, I knocked loudly for a long time. Lea finally stood in the vestibule just staring at me for what seemed like forever but finally unlocked the door. No words were spoken. I knew I had to go straight to my room and not say a word for fear she would come after me again. Needless to say, I did not sleep that night.

I continued to see Dave on and off for a few months, but he ultimately ended things abruptly, explaining that I was too inexperienced for him. I had been so desperate for love in my life, this relationship nearly destroyed me.

After the breakup. for some reason, Kimberly she began picking on me in school, I wonder if she ever really was a true friend or just jealous of the relationship I had with Dave and perhaps, she was glad it was over. She would sometimes egg on another friend of hers, Jackie, to come up to me out of the blue to start trouble. At times Jackie would walk right up to me and punched me in the face for no reason and a physical fight broke out between us. A large crowd circled around us in the hallway. This happened twice. Kimberly watched from behind the scenes and seemed as if she enjoyed being the instigator. For whatever reason, Kimberly was not very friendly and obviously had her own issues. We had sort of a love/hate friendship.

As for my studies throughout my freshman year, I honestly just lost interest. I was going through so much at home with Lea, it was impossible to concentrate on my academics. In school, I would just put my head down and sleep through my classes. Sometimes I would skip classes and be sent to resource rooms for detention. I was given detention and was suspended more times than I can count. Lea absolutely refused to get involved in what was going on in school saying that I wasted enough of her time in middle school. She told me I was to walk the five miles home from school if I got detention or was suspended. So, I did. Obviously, this high school was lost on me. I hated it and everyone in it. Little did I know my life was about to change forever.

Introducing Rita

From time to time, Lea and I would visit with her sister-in-law Rita (married to Lea's brother, Moe) and her daughter, my cousin Mary Ann in a nearby town. Mary Ann and I would spend a lot of time together in our preteen years. At eleven and twelve years old, it was a pivotal time in our lives as young ladies, and we became very close. Having a sense of what I was going through at the time, Rita and MaryAnn threw me a birthday party to help me feel better. I was turning 12 at the time and the party took place at their home in a neighboring town, with Mary Ann and her neighborhood friends. There was cake, punch and presents for me. Something I rarely received from Lea. I was shocked that at this party, Lea actually gave me five wrapped gifts, all brand-new Barbies. I was confused a bit as these were from Lea's prized collection. I wasn't sure if I was really allowed to open them, but I was told I could open one, so, I did. Mary Ann and I played with her dolls and my new Barbie. Interestingly, Lea ended up taking back the other four dolls. It was obvious that the multi-gift presentation was just for show.

After that day, it became evident that the relationship between Lea and Rita had become strained for some reason. We stopped seeing them for about three years for reasons I still don't understand today.

When I was in high school, Rita and MaryAnn moved to my town and Lea reached out to Rita. When I was 15 years old, Lea seemed desperate to get rid of me. That is when I went to live with Rita and her family. Although I finally lived in a home with a refrigerator and a working toilet, living there was still not ideal. The house was crowded with Rita, her husband, their daughter, MaryAnn and several extended family members. I was overcome with a mix of emotions, feeling abandoned, angry and sad. I was confused. To make matters worse, a truth bomb was about to land on me.

It was heartbreaking.

April 1985

Living with Rita and her family would end up backfiring on Lea because her long-kept secret was about to be revealed. I doubt Lea would ever have told me herself.

Oh boy. The truth. I remember that painful night like it was just, well, last night.

It was the spring of freshman year in high school and I had just moved in with Rita. I was 15. Despite not living with Lea anymore we continued our discord. There had been so much fighting and emotional and physical abuse, that I finally felt safe despite now living in a more crime-ridden area. Rita provided a small cot in the living room for me. Lea thought she got rid of me for good. However, Rita was about to pull the rug right out from under us.

"You and your mother need to talk." Rita would tell me often.
"About what?" I would ask.
"She'll know." She retorted.
I picked up the phone one night and dialed Lea's number.
"Mom, Rita says we need to talk." I told her.
"About what?" Lea hissed back.
"I don't know, but she says we should do it soon." I replied softly.
"Well, I don't know what she means and there's nothing to talk about!" She hung up. That was her usual way of ending a phone conversation with me.

Lea was doing everything she could to avoid the reality that was about to hit her, and it was going to hit hard. It didn't feel fair that I was being put under this pressure but even more so for her, who undoubtedly was feeling that same pressure. Personally, I knew better, and I sort of knew what it was about but Rita chose not to spill the beans just yet.

Lea had come over for dinner soon thereafter. We all ate, talked, and chatted much about nothing. It was after the plates were cleared and washed that Lea wanted to talk to her brother and Rita.

"Michelle, can you go outside for a little while? I need to talk to your uncle and Rita," she asked ever so nicely.

"Ok" I looked at her perplexed and began to go down the stairs. As I got halfway down, I could hear Lea's voice turn nasty and it made my skin crawl.

"I don't want you ever saying anything to Michelle" she said coldly. I imagined the disgusted look she had on her face.

"Lea, you know you have to tell her." Rita put her two cents right in.

As I walked down the stairs, I couldn't hear any more of their conversation, I just kept going and sat on the front stoop watching the cars race up and down the street. Deep down, I think I already knew.

I was not sure what the weekend was going be like after that. I was hoping to just hang out and do nothing and I was lucky. Things were quiet for a few days, and I went about those days as usual. One particular day not too long after Lea gave her warning to Rita, I had come home exhausted from school and just wanted to lie down. Except, Rita had other plans for me that night. She had had enough of Lea avoiding the truth and being in denial. Rita decided to take matters into her own hands.

Rita took me out to a fancy Italian bistro on the edge of town.

"Order anything on the menu including dessert!" She was in a generous mood and what teenager didn't want dessert!

I remember vividly that we had ordered spaghetti with meatballs, and I had a coke. Rita ordered a glass of red wine. We ate, talked about school and Rita felt what Lea was doing to me was wrong.

"What do you think my mother is doing so wrong?" I questioned, feeling my body starting to quiver.
"She is not telling you what you need to know" Rita quietly replied, sipped the last of her wine and proceeded to pay the bill.

Apparently, she was preparing to tell me everything in the car. She had a look in her eyes that I hadn't seen before. She was determined.

My heart was thumping out my chest. I had that nervous feeling that my life was about to be turned upside down pretty quickly. And it was. One thousand percent!

As we left the bistro and began driving to a local movie theater pub Rita began opening up, "I have a story to tell you."
"Ok, about what?" I asked. I suspected what was coming. C'mon heart, slow down.
"What I'm about to tell you, you cannot tell your Mother I told you!" she demanded. It was as if her voice went into slow motion.

She seemed so eager to tell me some story that I felt like I was having an out of body experience. I remember it almost word for word.

"Michelle, I'm sure you are aware that there are many Indian babies who have been given to other homes. Once upon a time there was this little Indian baby girl born on a reservation in Canada and was being given up for adoption. The birth mommy could not take care of her because there already were 7 or 8 other babies to feed. You were that little Indian baby she could not take care of, and nobody even knows who any of the fathers are." She thought that was funny. It wasn't.

I was mortified and numb. I didn't know what to say. Although I had seeds of suspicions already, I still had questions but didn't know how to ask but I asked anyway.

"Why couldn't Lea just tell me?"
"Because she didn't want to and do NOT tell your mother I told you."

I felt punched in the gut. I felt sick. I felt so many things and wanted to call Lea at once and scream at her and ask, "why couldn't YOU just tell me the truth like I had been asking for?!"

We arrived at the movie pub to finish our 'girls night out,' I could barely walk let alone watch the movie that was playing. Appropriately enough, the movie playing was The Terminator. I felt like I needed something to hold onto. Rita seemed proud of herself as she ordered me a Shirley Temple and herself another glass of wine. It was a tense evening for me anyway. After we left, we had another conversation about 'Indian babies' in the car.

"Indian babies are lucky to get adopted you know!" She laughed. Was I supposed to agree? I still sat quietly until a question came to me.
"Why are they so lucky?" I wanted to know.
"You were one of the lucky ones. You were so spoiled when your Daddy was alive. If you fell, you were picked up and coddled right away. You were given EVERYTHING." She was

vehement about my being spoiled. I didn't feel so lucky. I never did especially after Tom died.

So many things raced through my mind that sleep did not come easy for many days. I wasn't feeling so lucky.

It took me a couple of days before I even had the nerve to call Lea as I was supposed to after school, and she did not call me either. But I had to since we were in family therapy at the time, and I needed to confirm with her that we were going to therapy that week. I picked up the phone.

"Mom, we need to talk." I said very quietly. Her momentary silence filled the air.
"Who's been talking to you?" Was all she wanted to know. She knew it happened.
"No one, we just need to talk" I lied, my hand shaking the phone.
"Bullshit!" she exclaimed and slammed the phone down. She knew. Hell was about to blow its lid.

I figured Lea knew what was coming and she just didn't know how to stop it. Nothing was said on the phone about my adoption. I think she was waiting for me to talk to her first when I took the school bus to her house the next day to go to our session.

After calling Lea and telling her we needed to talk, our family therapy session day would soon be upon us. That day would be the big adoption reveal.

The therapy day came faster than I could blink my eyes. I know I barely slept for days. I went to school pretty much in a daze. When it came time to go to her house, the school bus seemed to have taken forever to get to the bus stop a block down the road from Lea's house.

I stepped off the school bus and walked to her house. I had this nervousness inside to the point of shaking and nausea.

When I finally reached the door, I wanted to run in the opposite direction because of my fear of saying anything to her. 'I can't do this,' I thought. 'I won't do this.' I decided right then and there as I was knocking on her door, that I wasn't going to say anything.

Lea had this 'if looks could kill' expression on her face when she let me in the house. She didn't say anything yet. Not one word. I went to my old room to just sit where I could be alone. I was scared to look at her, much less talk to her.

Finally, just before leaving for our therapy appointment, she came into the room.

"What do you want to talk to me about?" She asked, very sternly. I knew she was waiting for it. I think she felt weak too.

At first, I couldn't even speak, like there were nails in my throat.

"Oh, it was nothing." I managed to utter. I lied. I was literally afraid of this woman.

When she didn't like my answer, she blocked me in the doorway and confronted me. I thought for sure she was going to get physical at that moment, but she knew better as we were about to go out in public.

"WHAT DO YOU WANT TO TALK TO ME ABOUT!" She screamed in my face.

"Rita told me about my adoption!" I finally screamed back at her. We both froze.

Lea was pale.

For once, she did not know what to say. But you could see how pissed off she was. She had fire in her brown eyes.

"I planned on telling you when you turned 18." She said sharply.

"Why wait?" I was struggling to breathe.

"Because I thought you would be more mature and could handle it better."

Somehow that didn't make sense and still to this day, I don't think that she would have ever told me. I felt like she had taken that strap to me again. I was traumatized. These emotional bruises were not going away any time soon. Lea had disclosed that my entire adoptive family knew about my adoption, but they were sworn to secrecy around me. I was never to know anything. Lea did not trust anyone. I believe this might have been part of the reason that my adoptive family never came around.

"Do you know my real mother's name?" I asked, tears sliding down my cheeks.

"Yes, and you have a brother too," she said quietly, holding onto the frame of the door. I think she was about to faint at this point.

"What about all my other brothers and sisters?" I was confused.

"There is no one else. Your birth mother's name is Sharon and your brother's name is Michael." she shared.

"Did you ever meet Sharon?" I sobbed trying to catch my breath. I noticed Lea crying too.

"No, your father knew her family when he went to get you and bring you home." She explained.

I stood there not knowing what to say. It was shocking that she knew the names of my birth mother and brother.

"Do you have my adoption papers?" I asked.

"No, they are in Canada," she replied.

"Can you get a copy at least?" I begged.

"I don't know how." She responded. I was puzzled, even at the age of 15, I knew you needed some sort of paperwork to legally adopt a baby.

"Do you know who my birth father is?"

"No, that I don't know." She seemed almost apologetic as she wiped a few tears from her eyes.

"I actually have a letter that I received a few weeks ago from your brother looking for you." She pulled it out of the back of her desk where it was hidden in her bedroom. I was stunned. She grabbed more tissues to wipe her tears.

I quickly read the letter. Part of me believes that was the reason she no longer wanted me in the house.

March 15, 1985

Dear Mrs. Rice,

My name is Mike. My mother's name is Sharon. She has told me that I have a sister who is living with you in Connecticut. I would really like to be in contact with my sister, if you think that it would be a good idea. I am writing to you first to get your permission. Next, I would like to write to my sister. Could you please write me back with your answer? I would also like to have a picture of my sister, if this is possible. Thank you very much for helping me.

Yours sincerely,

Mike

I couldn't help but cry again after I read that letter. I always wanted a sibling. I never wanted to be alone. But I was.

Both Rita and Lea's versions of the "truth" would change me forever. It triggered me into so much more sadness and anger. I felt more broken, scarred, neglected and rejected than I had already been, and it took me down a long road of severe depression that I still deal with at times today.

That day of "truth" was a huge turning point in my relationship with Lea. A relationship that would be on and off again, and tumultuously rocky for the rest of our lives as I struggled with identity and trying to find a sense of belonging. I don't know if Rita was trying to do harm or not. She was a big believer that I should know the truth and she thought it was the right time and took the situation into her own hands. Rita felt it was her right to do so…but I was told never to tell Lea that she told me about the "truth." How does anyone lay that kind of pressure on a teenager? Against Rita's wishes, I did tell Lea. Let Lea be mad at someone else for once. And ohhh was she ever head-spinning mad!

On that day, we were running late, and we had to leave for our family therapy appointment. I didn't want to go. It was going to be ugly. All the "truth" had just come out like a vicious wave. I wasn't sure what to think – physically or emotionally. Our emotions were in turmoil and to be honest I don't know how Lea was able to drive the car. We both knew it would be better if we drove in silence, or at least I knew it would be better for my sake. I felt like she or I could snap at any moment.

As we arrived at the Community Guidance Center, the receptionist could see that we were both very upset. She saw the tears strolling down my face and immediately summoned our therapists. Once our therapists came and got us from the waiting area, we were taken into separate rooms as always but this time we both had to tell each of the therapists what was going on. I don't think my own therapist was surprised. She felt sorry about the way that I found out in a horrifying way. I could only imagine what Lea was telling her therapist. I imagine she felt sick more than anything having to tell anyone about her business, especially when it came time for us to meet all together to discuss the new monthly goals. They all felt that it was best if I did not pursue meeting my birth family. Lea looked desperate. However, in my own mind, that was not going to be the case. I was extremely determined to meet my birth mother. I sorely pretended to agree to hold off but deep in my heart I needed to know. I was going to know! After our individual sessions, we came together for our group meeting. Lea kept saying, "I don't want to deal with her anymore." She wouldn't say much more

45

than that. She would blame me for something, and all would be silent in our session together. What she didn't want to deal with this time was the truth I imagined. I think she knew this was coming and BOOM! Here it was. Life would become more upside down than we knew it.

We left the Community Guidance Center, again driving in silence. When we arrived back at Rita's house, I did not want Lea going after Rita in any way. I knew she wanted to as that fire of anger was still in her eyes and she might have gone after her, never realizing the consequences that might potentially have on me. It just did not make sense at that moment. I think Lea understood me although she just probably wanted to *kill* Rita. For my sake she held off.

Now that the secret was finally revealed, I felt like I already knew somehow. Although when a story is told by someone else and is completely stretched and exaggerated, the truth can become quite a shock. I felt waves of pain and numbness through my whole body that would last for decades.

"So, what happened? Tell me!" Rita confronted me as soon as I neared the door.
"Lea finally told me everything." I lied.
"She was under the pressure. Lea knew she didn't have a choice," Rita had gloated, "You look so tired."
"I am." I was matter of fact about that.

Later that night, lying on my cot, I woke up to Rita and her daughter, Mary Ann, sitting at the dinner table talking about what had happened. Mary Ann had no idea at that moment that it was her mother who had told me about things. She was only told that Lea had finally cracked under the pressure of having to tell me that I was adopted.

"You don't know how long I have wanted to tell you that you were adopted!" Mary Ann squawked.

"Really, oh." It was the only answer I could reasonably come up with without actually vomiting and spilling the beans about everything that really happened that day. I wanted so badly to say something to her, but I didn't dare. I was in a precarious situation.

"Yes, you needed to know Michelle." "It was about time." Mary Ann said.

If Rita only knew that I spilled the beans to my mother, she would have been mad and probably would have kicked me out that night. That would be for the near future to decide.

A couple of days went by after the whole truth came out; Lea did not call me nor did she check in with Rita. I figured she was disgusted and beyond herself at this point. I could barely function myself. It was a sad time for sure.

About two weeks later, Rita had handed me a letter asking me to leave their house and go back home. Home? Where was that? I was lost and broken.

May 18, 1985

Michelle Rice

Please be advised and inform your mother that you have until May 31, 85 to make other arrangements for living. We cannot and do not want to assume any more responsibility for you. We need the space and we have no room for you or any one at this time. If by the 31ˢᵗ of May, 85 you have not made other arrangements your clothes & you will be brought

to your mother's house.

Thank you.

Aunt Rita & Uncle Moe

Well wow! I once again felt like I had been hit by a truck. I felt rejected, again. They no longer wanted to care for me. I guess I couldn't blame them or her. I think Rita knew she was going to be in trouble at some point. In reality, the house was a bit too crowded. I didn't really want to leave but then again, it wasn't a choice and in the long run, I knew it was better that I leave. It was a good time to work on my 'plan' of somehow meeting my birth mother. I had a fantasy that she would just take me back and it would solve all my problems.

So, I went back to Lea's home to her dismay, but she knew she didn't have a choice. Though, I'm sure she would try and figure out some way to 'get rid of me' again. Things were quiet for a while – maybe for a few days. The house was still the same. Dirty and cluttered. Nothing changed. Lea seemed on edge, and she sensed I was on edge too but was probably hoping I would forget about everything. That would never happen.

It was during these few weeks that I had with her that I was going to ask so many questions which I had a right to. I was on a mission! I wasn't trying to cause trouble. I just wanted answers. She owed me at least that.

There was so much that Lea did not want me to know; always telling me it was 'none of my business' if I asked about her life or her finances. This time it *was* my business. She argued that I didn't need to know anything or, I love this part: she didn't know the answers to some of my questions.

For the next several weeks I asked questions.

"Mom, can we go to the reservation in Canada during summer vacation?" I asked quietly.

"No! I will never go back there!" She replied vehemently. "You cannot go there until you are an adult." She said in her nasty voice. I couldn't understand. I didn't want to understand.

"But why?" I asked.

"You don't need to know right now!" Her answers just stung me.

For days, I would just argue with her. I felt like I had a right to, and I know, without a doubt, I exhausted her with my questions about my birth family.

I had thought about what things might be like on the reservation. I wondered what Lea experienced as Tom's wife all the years before I was born. Was it ridicule in his family or just in general because she was a white woman? These are things I would begin to understand later in life.

Then I wondered about my birth family. I wondered about Sharon. I wondered about my birth father. What did they both look like. I wondered who my brother was. How big of a birth family did I have? Could my dreams actually come true that my family would rescue me and take me back? I didn't know.

After everything that had happened, I felt so different. I felt like another person. Maybe different is an understatement in the way that I felt. Maybe I felt traumatized, but I would carry this pain with me for years. I was incensed at the fact that my own 'mother', Lea, did not want to tell me the truth in the first place. She hid behind her own walls. What was she so afraid of? Maybe she just didn't know.

Maybe time would tell.

CHAPTER 6 – RETURN TO THE RESERVATION

May - September 1985 – Social and Cultural Struggles

From the moment I learned I was adopted, I struggled with who I was. I began fantasizing about meeting my birth family. I wondered what they looked like. Did I look like them?

I wondered what life on the reservation was like. I wondered how native people lived and what Canada look liked? All these questions and no answers yet. Rita had her theory about my birth family. According to her, my family was poor, impoverished and couldn't feed a family of seven or eight babies. Rita was known to dramatize stories. I guess Rita felt like she had to take matters into her own hands because she knew Lea would always lie to me. My entire adoptive family never realized the detriment it would cause me for years. Since Lea had lost respect for Rita and I was still tangled in Lea's web, I didn't see much of Rita or other family members after that.

Regardless, I knew I had to find my roots. Lea refused initially to let me go to Canada telling me I could go when I was 18. I was not having it. I was stubborn and very determined to make contact with my birth mother, Sharon.

Lea was not thrilled about me making calls, but I wanted to, needed to, and was determined to.

"Mom, I want to call and get Sharon's phone number." I said.

"No, I don't want you making any calls to Canada." She replied.

"But why?" I cried.

"Because I said so!" She waved her finger in my face.

"And if you touch that phone, I will cut the phone wires so you can't make any calls!" She yelled.

She knew she really couldn't do that and while she made her threats, I think the look on my face told her that I was not backing down anytime soon so she backed off. Wasn't I already feeling enough anguish? She knew I was wild enough to go elsewhere and finish my plan of execution. I'm sure if I went back to Rita's just for a few hours, Rita would have let me make the calls that I needed. But something changed at that moment with Lea. She suddenly threw up her hands and said,

"Do what you want!"

It would be an expensive call, but I had no choice. I picked the phone.

"Canada 411, how can I help you?" the operator asked.

"I would like the number for Sharon Smith in Kahnawake please," I asked.

"I don't seem to have a number for that name, Miss. Is there another name?" She asked.

"I'm not sure. Hold on." I held my hand over the receiver asking Lea if there was another name I should go by.

"I don't know." Lea was exasperated.

"I don't know, but maybe if you look up S. Smith in Kahnawake please? I pleaded.

"Here is a number for you," the operator gave me the number and I wrote it down as fast as I could.

"Thank you," I said as I quickly hung up.

Lea was not happy with me.

"Are you done now?" She rebuked.

"Not yet." I was nauseous and wanted to throw up.

I waited a couple of days before I made that next call. There was a constant pit in my stomach telling me 'not yet' and I needed to tread lightly at home. Those couple of days went by and I finally picked up the phone and just dialed the number. Lea nervously paced in the kitchen while smoking like a chimney. She was not expecting me to pick up that phone so soon.

One ring. Two Rings.

"Hello?" a nice lady answered.

"Hi, my name is Michelle and I'm calling from Connecticut. May I please speak to Sharon Smith?" I asked nervously but politely.

"Eh? Sorry dear, you have the wrong number." The lady replied.

"Oh. This was the number I was given. I am calling for my birth mother, Sharon, and thought this would be the number," I nervously explained.

"Really, eh? Here is a number you should call. Are you ready?" She asked.

"I am." I replied, pen in hand.

She graciously gave me a different phone number and wished me luck. I needed it.

I was grateful. She was such a nice lady. I would eventually learn that she had the same name as my biological grandmother, Mary. I would have loved to meet this woman who gave me the phone number to thank her, but I never got the chance.

I waited another day or two before I called Sharon. That pit in my stomach was stronger. I figured my attempt for that night was enough. Lea barely muttered a word while I was trying to connect with Sharon.

When I finally called the number, I was shaking.

One ring. Two rings. Two and a half rings.

"Hello?" it sounded like a young boy answered. I would later find out it was my cousin Kurt about the same age as me.
"Hello. Is Sharon there?" I stumbled.
"Uhhhh, no. Can I take a message?" he asked politely.
"I'm Michelle, Sharon's daughter." I blurted out.
Silence.
"Hold on please..." he muffled the phone, speaking to someone else in the background.
"What?!" a startled voice in the background could be heard and apparently grabbed the phone from him.
"Who is this?!" the woman's voice asked.
"My name is Michelle. I am looking for Sharon. I believe she is my birth mother?" I quivered. I thought she might say I have the wrong number or just hang up on me but oh to the contrary.
"Oh my God!" she exclaimed. "Hello Michelle, I am ... your... your...your grandmother, Mary. I can't believe it's really you!" She sounded like she was catching her breath.
"Oh wow! Can I speak to Sharon? Is she there?" I questioned.
"She is out tonight, but I promise to have her call you." she said. She proceeded to ask me how I was and hoped to talk to me some more. I hoped for that too.

I can only imagine what my grandmother told Sharon when she came home that night. Like me, I doubt anyone in that household slept. I waited a long sleepless night and a long day through school but that next night, the phone rang. I had a feeling it was for me. I shakily answered the phone.

"Hello?"
"Is this ... Michelle?" A woman's voice sounded quietly nervous. It was Sharon. To finally hear her voice was surprisingly lifting.

"Hi, yes this is me." I replied excitedly. I couldn't believe my birth mother said my name!

"This is Sharon. How are you? She asked. You could tell she was nervous too.

"I'm good. How are you?" I politely asked back. Being 15, I guess I wasn't a good conversationalist.

"I'm nervous but am happy to talk to you." She laughed.

We talked for at least 15 – 20 minutes. She never questioned why I called or what I wanted. There was nothing I needed except to make a connection with her. I believe she knew that.

We seemed to be at ease with each other instantly. We talked about my life in Connecticut, my school, and my friends. She told me how many aunts, uncles, and cousins I had. I learned I had a big family with one brother. Not the seven or eight siblings Rita had assumed in her story to me.

It was the general banter of getting to know each other. I know she was happy to connect. She said she always wanted to find me. I asked her if she had my adoption papers there and she admitted I was never legally adopted. I was shocked.

This news did not seem to surprise Lea, which made me think she knew that, as well. My actual birth and baptismal certificate was forged to show that I was born in Connecticut and Lea and Tom were my birth parents. I did not know at the time but this would create many problems growing up. Ugh.

I think Sharon always thought about the day we would reconnect. I think she dreamed of it. Maybe not so soon, but one day. Sometimes I think in hindsight, I should have waited until I was an adult for us to reconnect, but I was really hellbent on realizing my 'dream.' The dream of my birth family 'rescuing' me.

By continuing our phone conversations in the days and weeks that followed, much to my delight we seemed to be bonding at last. Sharon even told me she loved me during our second call. Cue the tears.

We talked about my coming up to Canada to meet the family at some point. I really wanted to visit that summer after talking to her, but I knew Lea would have an issue with that. I would have to tread lightly around the subject, fearing her wrath.

I decided to write to my brother, Mike, after reading his letter and talking to Sharon. I told him I had just recently found out about him as well and how happy I was to know that I had a brother. He would write me back and tell me how happy he was to find me, about how he wanted to join the Army or go back to school. He wanted to go to welding school to become an ironworker just like many other family members. He sent me a picture of himself. He was a handsome young man. I had shown his picture to a friend of mine who instantly developed a crush. Good looks apparently run in the family. My brother had just turned 17 and was in shock when he found out he had a sister. My brother was excited that I was thinking of coming to Canada to meet the family. He had called me twice so we could talk. I felt that was very nice at the time.

I had always hoped that my brother, Mike and I would become close, having that brother and sister bond, but that would not be the case. We are two very different people in life. As it turned out, my brother had a substance abuse problem and was in a detention center for juveniles in Canada at the time we talked.

The thought of meeting Sharon sooner rather than later was really weighing on me, and I begged Lea to let me go. After arguing non-stop, Lea finally agreed. I'm pretty sure I wore her down. I think her conclusion was that this was her way to 'get rid of me' again. I think Lea resented me in that moment.

Sharon had said on our initial phone call that it was never her intention to give me up, but she didn't have a choice. She always thought of me which would be confirmed by other family members. She would elaborate more of the 'why' in person one day.

After another call with Sharon and my grandmother, I had asked if I could come up that summer to visit and they were thrilled they would finally meet me. We had made plans that I would leave the day after school ended for the summer. I would take a bus to Montréal. I described what I would be wearing, a black and red checkered skirt and a white blouse. As the days went on from that late spring until the last day of school, I was getting more excited and anxious at the same time. Things at home were not great. They were more tense. Lea did not have much in the way of luggage, so I had many duffle bags of clothes. Lea seemed to be in a hurry to get me packed up. She was acting odd all week.

Before the big trip, Sharon sent me a couple of letters with pictures of family, and I would send her a couple of letters with pictures as well. Lea initially refused to give me some school pictures she purchased but again relented. I argued that Sharon should know what I look like when I get off the bus.

During the planning phase of my impending trip to Canada, I remember accompanying Lea to the apartments for rent collection. Some of the tenants would ask me about school and what my plans were for the summer. I said, "I was going on a trip to Canada. I'm going to meet my 'real' mother." This bewildered some people, but others seemed to understand. This bothered Lea to her core, and she would confront me about it. When we got home that night, she started yelling at me and chased me with that leather strap, but I turned around and stared at her ready to take the blows. But oddly, she didn't strike me this time. I think she would have if I hadn't stood right up to her, almost daring her to do it.

"You know you don't have to say you're visiting your 'real' mother in Canada" she seemed mournful.

"What am I supposed to say? Isn't Sharon my 'real' mother? I asked.

"No, I am your REAL mother," she snapped back.

"Um, didn't Sharon give birth to me?" I quizzed her sarcastically.

Lea looked livid. She had no answer. It was obvious that I exuded an intense energy at that moment. She backed away.

On the last day of school, teachers and friends wished me well. That night, Sharon called to confirm my trip and what time I would be arriving.

"Hi Michelle!" Sharon sounded excited.

"Hi there!" I was excited too.

"I wanted to confirm, you are coming up here tomorrow?" She asked.

"Yes, I should arrive by 5:30 tomorrow at the bus station in Montreal. I leave Hartford at 7:45 a.m." I explained.

"Ok, good! Get some good sleep tonight." She seemed so sweet.

"Ok, you too!" I replied knowing that neither of us would sleep that night.

It would be a long, sleepless night tossing and turning on my cot, the only bed I ever knew in Lea's home. What was my trip going to be like? I'm going to another country. I was a bundle of nerves and excitement all rolled up into one! Lea had no words for me that night. Not even an "I'll miss you" or "I love you."

The next morning, a sunny day, we headed out to the bus station, and Lea drove quietly. Still, not a word was spoken. I tried to have some conversation with her, but really it was no use.

"So, Mom, will you miss me?" I asked quietly.

"Not really. I need some quiet time." She would look at me rather seriously. I tried to be understanding so I just let it go.

"Well, ok. But I'll miss you. I love you, Mom. Do you love me?" I asked, hoping to hear the answer I longed to hear from her.

"I guess so." She was not so pleasant. Sigh. It was what it was.

We arrived at the Hartford bus station, which was in the middle of the busy city and not in a great area. We realized I had missed the initial bus I was supposed to be on. Lea had to quickly exchange the ticket for the next bus that was about to leave soon after. When I looked at the ticket and realized that it wasn't a round trip ticket, my heart dropped. I looked at Lea and asked why. She was exasperated and said she would send me a return ticket home at the end of the summer. I believed her. I watched her walk fast back to her car without so much as looking back or waving at me.

As the bus driver loaded all my duffle bags in the cargo-hold of the big blue Greyhound bus, I stepped up the big steps ready to go to Montréal. It was big enough to carry 56 people. There seemed to be people from all walks of life that were getting on this bus with me. The seats were rather uncomfortable and had worn red leather and cloth upholstery. I chose a seat somewhere in the middle by the window so I could watch the world go by as we were driven to our next stop. I remember the bus was not filled with people yet. I could hear people talking and laughing. I didn't have much to do except put on a radio/cassette walkman that I had brought with me so that I could listen to my music.

Our bus would make 5 stops, one in Albany, Syracuse, Plattsburgh, the Canadian border and of course, Montreal. We had to make a transfer to another bus in Albany because my bus had an engine issue. So, we were delayed to the dismay of many passengers. I didn't know how to react being my first trip, so I just went with the flow. I made a collect call to Lea which she wasn't pleased about. I explained that we were going to be delayed due to engine issues and I asked her to call Sharon to explain the situation. Lea begrudgingly agreed. She had already called Sharon that morning to say I had to get on a later bus and would arrive later than anticipated.

After being transferred to the other bus, the bus driver was rather frustrated and said he needed to smoke and hoped that we didn't mind. Some passengers asked if they could smoke too, and he agreed. Oh, the eighties! So, the entire bus became filled with cigarette smoke. I felt sick. It was not easy to ingest this, so I just laid down across the two seats until the next stop. I managed to doze off for a while.

This was my first trip by myself, and I was nervous, maybe even a bit scared. I was only 15 years old. This new adventure was a bit overwhelming all of sudden, but I think that was normal. My life was about to change. The bus trip included an hour at the border with the border agents questioning many people about their travel paperwork including myself but nonetheless they let me in. I talked to the bus driver outside after using the washroom at the border and I asked him how much longer we had before we got to Montreal and he said, "Oh we have a little over an hour to go young lady." Ugh.

When I finally reached the bus station in beautiful downtown Montreal, I was exhausted. The sun was just setting over the cityscape. There are so many tall buildings in Montreal. I never really knew how vast that city was.

It took me a while to get off the bus as there were many people in front of me gathering their belongings from overhead. When I finally disembarked, I saw this old lady with short red curly hair running up to me with her arms spread wide to hug me with all her might. She had pure joy and tears on her face. I'll never forget the emotion. This must be my grandmother, Mary.

"Grandma?" I exclaimed! I held my arms out and hugged her. I knew instantly this was my grandmother, Mary.
"Yes, it's me!" She cried pulling me close, squeezing me so tight and kissing me on the cheek.

Right behind her were two young boys. My brother Mike and my cousin Kurt. I nervously shook their hands. As I did, I made eye contact with my birth mother, Sharon. I couldn't help but notice how beautiful she was. She was teary eyed and looked relieved when I saw her. We hugged each other tightly.

"It's really you?" I asked.

"It is." Sharon replied shyly.

"I'm so glad to be here." I began tearing up.

My new family appeared to be happy. We all seemed to be a bit relieved.

After our initial reunion, we took a break from all the hugging, threw my duffle bags into the car and we went into the bar located inside the busy station. I had some peanuts and some seltzer while the others had a beer. They just wanted me to relax after my long trip. Sharon and my grandmother both kept staring at me, petting my arm and calling me beautiful and gorgeous. This was something I could get used to as I had never been truly complimented by Lea. As we sat and talked, I found myself staring at Sharon. I couldn't believe my birth mother was sitting across from me.

"So, Michelle, did you have a good bus trip?" my grandmother asked.

"It was long but yes, good," I replied.

"How was your last day of school?" Sharon asked.

"Okay." I didn't know really how to respond.

"Lea called to say you were going to be delayed." Sharon informed me.

"I knew she would." I was waiting to hear what else Lea might have said.

"Lea said you like Kentucky Fried Chicken." Sharon said. "She said you had a good appetite and aren't fussy." Nope, I wasn't fussy.

As we were chatting, I was told I was going to stay at my grandmother's house for the summer as that is where Sharon lived.

When it came time to leave the bus station, we all piled into the car that Sharon had borrowed to pick me up. We traveled away from the cityscape of Montreal and approached the Kahnawake Reserve. I felt like I had seen some of the area before. Maybe I was having flashbacks as a toddler when Tom, my father, took me there before he died. As the sun was setting, I remember going over the Mercier Bridge, seeing the roaring St. Lawrence Seaway/River and all the scenery around. You could see the cityscape of the south side of Montreal which was breathtaking as the sun set on the landmark buildings. I remember seeing the Kahnawake town Catholic Church steeple. It was all very surreal. I remember seeing homes that really didn't look any different than any other town except for the one fun fact that still is today, there are no physical street signs. None of the roads had names. Everyone has a post office box for their mail. There were/are historic homes still standing which were neat to see and I think some of the landmarks were explained to me but I don't quite remember them. The local Church name really stood out as that is where I was baptized and recalled seeing the Church's name on my birth / baptismal certificate. Their local hospital had not been built yet in 1985 but was about to go into construction.

We drove through the reserve to another little town called Chateauguay. We went to the local Kentucky Fried Chicken where a load of food was purchased. I remember joking that there must be an army waiting for us. Everyone laughed. It seemed to break some of the ice. As we finally made it to my grandmother's house, there were lots of people awaiting my arrival.

Greeting me were Sharon's sisters, Aunt Arlene, Aunt Sue, Aunt Sue's other two sons, Wayne and Ryan and a few others that I can't quite recall. Surprisingly, no pictures were taken. It was a festive evening. Everyone seemed to spoil me with food, soda, and attention. I was exhausted but really happy.

Through dinner and afterwards, I would try to get to know my brother a little bit as he would have to go back to the detention center the next day. He had alcohol/substance abuse issues coupled with some trouble that he had gotten into. I never asked what happened. I never judged him. I was just glad that he was getting the help he needed at the time. It couldn't have been easy living in a detention center. We hung out together that night with our cousins, getting to know each other a little bit more.

"Are you tired Michelle?" Mike asked me.

"A little bit." I didn't want to seem like a party pooper.

"What grade are you in now?" Mike asked.

"I'll be in tenth grade this September." I replied.

"Do you get good grades?" He was really interested.

"Not too bad," I didn't want to totally explain any troubles I had.

"I plan to go back to school myself and then I want to join the military" he said.

"That's great, keep going on that." I encouraged him.

Mike held my hand, so happy to have a sister. He and I both hoped for a long-lasting brother and sister bond.

Sharon would check on me throughout the evening asking if I needed anything. I was overwhelmed by all the attention.

Later, it seemed as though everybody in the extended family and some friends in town had come over to meet me that night. This was one big family. Oh my. Community seemed to be everything to everyone.

Sharon was grinning from ear to ear when answering the phone if anyone called asking if I had finally arrived and she kept telling people how beautiful I was as she looked down the stairs to the basement where we were gathered. She told the callers how happy she was to have me there. She seemed to be glowing with pride!

Sharon's boyfriend at the time, Aimee, had arrived to meet me later that night. He was this boisterous French man who lived in a one-room shack on the reservation working for the local garage as a tow truck driver. He appeared to be a very nice man, but I would come to find out later he could be a bit devilish at times. He was also a very generous man. If he was drinking as he often did, he would sing opera or dance. He was quite the one-man show. There was never a dull moment when Aimee was around. He seemed to make Sharon happy.

I finally lied down on the living room couch because I was so exhausted from my travels but so wound up being in a strange place, in a totally different country. I remember Sharon coming in to sit on the arm of the couch and she started crying saying how sorry she was. I knew from stories that people told me over the years after we met, that Sharon always talked about me and would remember me on my birthday wondering what I would be doing. Sharon wanted to find me, but it was my grandmother, Mary, who told her to leave it alone in my best interest. I remember me telling her that it was all ok. There was so much emotion that night and it would continue through my entire visit that summer.

I knew I needed sleep that night. Sharon had bought me a new nightgown. I was to share my grandmother's bedroom in a small twin bed, which was bigger than the cot I was used to at home. When my grandmother finally came in to go to bed, she lied down in the bed next to mine and immediately started to snore, loudly. I remember getting up and opening the door staring at my Auntie Sue and Sharon sitting at the kitchen table.

"Are you ok Michelle?" Auntie Sue was concerned.
"I think there's a lion in my room." I said sleepily.

They couldn't contain their laughter. Grandma could snore with the best of them. I miss that snore. The snore heard 'round the world'. That was the snore that I would inherit as I became older and now resonates as to what I know as the family trait along with the other proclivities of our genes.

My grandmother's modest white house stood on its own corner not too far from the riverbanks of the St. Lawrence Seaway. She owned another house behind it, but it was unoccupied. You entered my grandmother's house from the side and came up a few steps into the kitchen. The home had your typical living room, kitchen, one bathroom and three bedrooms on the first floor. There was the basement which seemed to be the hangout place for the kids to sleep and watch tv. You could always find my grandmother sitting at her kitchen table, either talking with whoever was there, be it guests or family and/or preparing meals. There was always something cooking. During the day, if she made soup, she would call her children and say "soup's on." They would all stop over for lunch.

At night, I would hear the ships' horns as they were passing through the St. Lawrence Seaway, and I'd often get up and watch the ships sail from the window of my grandmother's bedroom. It was nice to see their lights in the middle of the night. If it was early evening, I sometimes would take a walk over to the riverbank and watch the ships up close. I could see the lights of Old Montreal at night from there. It was such a charming city to see.

As I spent time in Kahnawake throughout the summer, I began to get to know many people. I would take morning walks near the house, hang out with some cousins, go grocery shopping with my grandmother and have lunch with her at a local café where she would speak Mohawk with her friends if they joined us. I figured they were talking about me or...just gossiping. LOL! I didn't understand the Mohawk language.

I would also meet a boy that summer in Canada. As usual I longed for a meaningful relationship but that was not in the cards. He was a nice enough guy that I met at a party with my cousins in a house behind my grandmother's, but, despite an intimate evening together, I never saw him again after that.

The family soon learned that I was not very domestic. Lea never taught me how to clean a house or cook. Sharon and Mary tried to teach me but somehow being domestic just never clicked with me.

However, I was not inept at doing other things. I helped my grandmother stack boxes in the basement, I helped the elderly woman next door with her groceries, and I would even babysit for a friend of Sharon's on Friday nights.

On some Sundays Sharon, Aimee and I would go to a lake in Isle La Mott in Vermont for a swim and picnic. Other times we would go to the horse races at the old Blue Bonnet in Montreal. I remember having Aimee place a bet for me where I won $600.00. That was like a fortune to me as a kid then. I was so excited. I had some spending money for a while. I just wasted it on things like make-up and shoes that I'm sure I didn't need at the time.

While there were good times being had, I was also experiencing a lot of anger and depression deep inside. I'm not sure why I was feeling the way I was, but I didn't let on. I had a birth family that was so happy to have me back even if for a short time. They showed me nothing but compassion and joy. Could this be what love is? Sad to say at 15 years old, I never really knew that motherly love. They shared their home with me freely. We had fun attending a couple of wrestling matches and going to concerts such as Foreigner and Tina Turner. You would think I'd never want to leave Canada, yet somehow, despite my life with Lea I started becoming homesick.

At first, when I wanted to use the phone to call Lea, I asked my grandmother's permission to call home and I was told yes, but not to stay on too long because of the expense. In typical fashion, Lea would usually be less than receptive towards me when I called but every so often, she seemed like she missed me. It was confusing. She reminded me about my dog, Pepper, and how she wanted "to get rid of the dog." Pepper acted like my protector when I was home, so I felt gut punched. She knew how much Pepper meant to me. I felt the need to get home now.

By the end of the summer, I was calling Lea every day without my grandmother's permission, sometimes twice a day. I wanted to come home but also wanted to be sure Pepper was still there. I had been fighting with Lea to send me the bus ticket back and she wouldn't. The time to go back to school was growing closer. Then one day she told me to stay where I was because she didn't want me back. I never told my birth family anything about what was going on at home. I probably should have. I was just so angry at everything. To realize Lea had turned tables on me once again was just pushing me further over the edge.

I ran my grandmother's phone bill up pretty high. Grandma was disappointed in me. I think I disappointed a lot of people then. It was an act of anger, just not caring…I felt like I was entitled to do that, and nobody should question me. How wrong I was. I later learned that the phone bill was over $200.00, and I had no money left at that time. Grandma eventually called Lea about a month after my return home to tell her about the bill. Lea didn't seem to care, and I heard her say "I'll talk to her." All she ever said to me about it was, "you ran up your grandmother's phone bill." She said nothing else.

I turned 16 in Canada. There was no birthday party but there were some gifts. My grandmother had bought me some clothing which was appreciated. Sharon had given me a beautiful gold band ring that I had seen her wear and I fell in love with it. She gave it to me with love and told me to hold on to it. I would wear it all the time and think of Sharon and all that she shared with me. Years later between many moves, I lost the ring. It broke my heart to lose that precious piece of my birth mother that meant so much to me.

While I don't remember every moment of that summer of 1985, it was a trip that I wouldn't forget. Lea finally did send me that bus ticket at the very end of the summer.

On my last night in Kahnawake, Sharon and I had a night to ourselves. She had given me her own suitcase to use and helped me pack. We had dinner and she decided she wanted to take a drive with me one last time.

She drove me around the reservation, and we talked about my going back home, and going back to school (school was important to her as she didn't finish school herself). We drove towards the seaway, watching the water ripple, the sunset, and the lights flicker over Montreal. She stopped and turned the car off. Leaving was going to be so hard for both of us. She started to speak, her voice breaking.

"Michelle, I hope you forgive me," she begged. Honestly, there was no forgiveness to be had.

"It's okay Sharon. I know you didn't give me up to hurt me." I tried to reassure her, but I was getting emotional too. I didn't know what I wanted at that point.

"After I gave you up, I went through the hardest time in my life. There would be nights where I would just drive around and find a quiet spot and just cry." She choked on her tears.

"But now you have me back." I reassured her.

"I'm glad. I want you to go back, be good and do good in school. Ok?" She wanted nothing but the best for me.

"I will and I'll be back next summer to visit" I hoped I would be able to come back.

We both cried for a while as we held each other. Neither of us wanted to let go. It would be another sleepless night in anticipation of my leaving.

The next morning was quiet. We had breakfast and it was time to leave for the bus station. I hugged everyone goodbye. My grandmother was emotional and wanted to talk as well. She had been wanting to say something all summer.

"I'll miss you, my granddaughter." Grandma would choke up.

"I'll miss you too Grandma." I said.

"I hope you understand why I made Sharon give you up." She offered.

"I think so." I replied.

"I was raising your brother and I couldn't raise you too. Your mother was too young and not ready to raise you." She explained that it was too much at the time, especially financially. She felt that Tom was a good choice as a father for me.

"Grandma, its ok. I get it". I didn't want to talk about it anymore.

Truth be told, my grandmother made a huge impact on me in a positive way just by opening her heart to me. I loved her spirit.

While saying goodbye at my grandmother's I spoke with my brother, still at the detention center, and said goodbye over the phone. That was hard but we knew we'd see each other again. We promised we would write to each other, but letters were few between the two of us.

I got into the same car that Sharon borrowed to pick me up at the bus station in Montreal. As the car started rolling down the roads, I watched the town I had gotten to know slowly disappear from my sight and give way to the bus station in Montreal. Once at the bus station, Sharon waited with me until my bus was called over the loudspeaker. My suitcase was loaded into the cargo hold and then it was time for me to get on the bus. I quickly hugged and kissed Sharon, promised I would call once I got home and stepped up on the bus steps, blowing more kisses to her. It felt like the same bus that had driven me into Montreal was now taking me back to Connecticut. Same worn red leather/upholstery seats with an occupancy for 56. The bus was at passenger capacity, so I needed to make sure I found my same window seat in the same row. I sat down and was able to wave until we pulled out of the station and into the city towards the highway.

Throughout the entire long bus ride home, I was in deep thought about the summer. There were so many emotions, so many memories, swirling in my mind. This was the first time I felt compassion, joy and love from family members. I met some amazing people who all welcomed me with open arms. Amazing community. Yet, somehow, I was still angry, sad and torn between the two worlds.

While it was a coming-of-age experience for me, I still wondered why my birth family never connected me to any of Tom's family still living in Kahnawake at the time. I should have asked, but I didn't. My grandmother even said she knew his family. I often wondered if Lea had something to do with it. I'll never know.

When I arrived back in Connecticut, I experienced bouts of culture shock and couldn't seem to gain control of my emotions. I realize now that it was the native traditions and loving native community of the reservation that were suddenly taken away from me, again. I suddenly longed for my Native American community.

In the end, I'm sure I made my memorable mark on my birth family as they did to me.

CHAPTER 7 – BACK TO MAYHEM

September 1985

It was a long drive back to Hartford. Nine and a half hours long. The bus did not go through New York this time, but through Vermont. The scenery was gorgeous. I truly enjoyed the ride this time, yet I was nervous about what awaited me back home. We stopped several times along the way to drop passengers off or pick them up. Those stops helped to stretch our legs before we reached my final destination.

Having to go back to Lea at the end of a beautiful summer in Canada was not easy. It hurt that she told me on the phone that she did not want me back. She probably gave in to sending me the return bus ticket because she knew, even though I was 16 years old, I would somehow find my way back. I purposely kept this from my birth family as I did not want them to know about the troubled waters at home. I thought Lea may have reconsidered her feelings about things and really did want me back. I had nowhere else to go anyway. Looking back, I should have just stayed in Canada, and I should have never kept this a secret from my birth family.

I arrived back at the Hartford Greyhound Bus Terminal in Connecticut, exhausted. I could see Lea sitting in her station wagon, smoking her cigarette, looking rather serious or disappointed that I made it back. She didn't get out of the car until I stepped off the bus to retrieve the suitcase that Sharon had

71

given me. I wondered if Lea would notice that I no longer had her dirty old torn duffle bags that I left with. She never said anything about the suitcase.

"I have a surprise for you." Lea said from behind me.

There were no hellos or welcome back greetings. Not even a hug. She forced a smile. She rarely smiled. Her dark eyes were distant. I had chills yet I was hopeful at the same time.

"What? Did you redo my bedroom?" I begged, secretly praying that she did.

"You'll see," she said in a real monotone voice.

"Aren't you even glad I'm back?" I stared at her. She never answered me.

I had hoped she would be in a good mood and had fixed the house. Maybe she changed my bedroom to something better than the hazardous squalor I had lived in. Maybe my prayers would finally be answered. We stopped to eat, and I kept asking her what the surprise was but was always met with the same response "you'll see," She was not even remotely interested in my trip. She never asked me any questions about it. She could tell I was different and while I was numb to her reaction of me being back, I was exhausted but still hoping for the best.

We finally got back to the house and once I walked inside, I realized nothing had changed. The hoarding had gotten worse. I didn't think it was possible. Close your eyes and picture black mold, mildew, dirt and dust everywhere. The mold and mildew had grown up the walls in the kitchen and the stench of old ashtrays and a dirty toilet burned my nose. I needed to use the bathroom but was scared to step one foot in. Ugh. I had just come from a nice clean home.

My bedroom door was closed but she egged me on to open the door.

"Go ahead, open the door!" she urged.

Still praying for a nice surprise and maybe the start of change perhaps through the house, I smiled and opened the door. To my shock, the musty smelling room was filled with boxes stacked from floor to ceiling. Boxes that were full of junk from her hoard she had collected. Boxes that weren't mine. My stomach was queasy, and I was numb. Again. Even the little cot I slept on was gone. My bedroom was no more.

"I moved *my* things in here and your cot is not in here" Lea snapped, "I'm taking this room over, this is not your room or home. I don't want you here anymore!" Lea looked at me disgusted.

"I don't understand!" I started to break down. After a long summer and a long trip home, I was too tired to play her game that moment, but she forced the situation.

"Your behavior is awful and you're not loyal to me as your mother!" She spit at me.

"What are you talking about?!" I cried.

"You're not going to school tomorrow. You're leaving tomorrow!" She was adamant.

"What do you mean Mom?" I was exhausted and just wanted to go to bed. To my horror, I really had no place to sleep in that house.

"We have a therapy session in the morning, they're going to decide what to do with you!"

"But why?" I cried over and over.

"You know why!" She spat again.

I really didn't know. I just knew she didn't want to handle the truth or listen to me.

"What about my dog?!" I screamed, after seeing Pepper tied to a kitchen cabinet handle.

"I'm getting rid of her!" She screamed back.

"Are you giving her away?" I was nearly hysterical.

"No, I'm going to put her down!" She had a glean in her eyes that made me want to lunge at her. My poor dog was whining in the kitchen and I wasn't allowed to see her or hold her.

"Mom, you can't throw me and Pepper out like this!" I screamed and realized I needed to say something fast to get her to stop in her tracks.

I took a deep breath, dropped my head, and whimpered "You can't throw me out, at least not now!"

Lea went pale. "Why not?!"

"Mom, I didn't want to tell you like this." I had to think of something quickly.

"I think I'm pregnant!" I stood there waiting for her to react. She suddenly became quiet. She looked scary. My eyes searched for anything that might protect me if she had come after me physically, but I think she was too stunned.

"What do you mean you think you're pregnant?" Not a sound could be heard when she questioned me.

"Just what I said. I think I may be pregnant. Where do I go from here Mom?" I asked her sarcastically. I was so tired. I just needed her to stop.

I had lied to her, held my breath, started to shake as I didn't want to reveal that I had a short-lived fling while in Canada, but I felt cornered. I just needed her to stop all of what she was trying to do to me.

After I blurted out the news that I might be pregnant, Lea finally said she had enough. She gave me a small sleeping bag to sleep in without a pillow and said that she was going to bed. She was disgusted. I was simply trying to save my life and my dog's life. I knew I needed to stay there to protect Pepper. Despite the turmoil, sleep was a welcome relief. As I lay in the corner on a dirty carpet, I closed my eyes with a few tears flowing down my cheeks, I wondered why this woman hated me so much. Did she hate herself too?

The next morning, I felt like my head was about to fall off with a pounding headache. Therapy was scheduled for later that morning. Lea did not offer me breakfast and I was afraid to open any cabinets without permission. Nothing was said. It was a quiet morning. I untied Pepper and took her outside for a bit. As she licked my legs and wagged her tail, I realized my dog was the only being that ever showed me consistent love. Soon after, I asked Lea if I could at least open my suitcase to get some clothes out. She agreed and I went to wash up in the filthy bathroom. I felt even worse.

We got in the car, and we were silent the whole way over to the therapists' office. The car was filled with the nauseating stench of old cigarettes in the ashtray. When we arrived at the clinic for our return therapy session, the receptionist once again could see how upset I was just by the look on my face.

She was very nice asking how my summer went in Canada, and she could see the look on Lea's face as if to say, "how dare you ask her anything!" It was a very uncomfortable moment.

The two therapists came, Dina and Mary, came in and took us into one office where we could have a full family therapy session. I was asked many questions about my trip, and I answered most of them. When I discussed how accepting my Canadian family was, I wanted to be honest and say that it felt great, but I couldn't openly say that with Lea in the room. The one question I hated being asked was "And how did that make you feel?" I wanted to scream.

Lea began to rant about me and my 'bad behavior'. She hadn't seen me in over two months. It became obvious to the therapists that Lea did not want me home anymore. I believe they were now afraid for my safety. I would find out years later that that the therapists had called State Department of Children and Youth Services the month before requesting placement upon my return from Canada.

Lea continued to stand on her soapbox suddenly accusing me of stealing from her home over the summer…when I wasn't even there! She actually thought I was sending people to watch the house while I was gone. Her paranoia was rearing. She described cars being parked along the road casing the house to break in. Did she forget we lived next to a public water reservoir where people often came to swim and fish?

I was hoping she had a change of heart about me. Afterall, when I found out about my adoption, she did admit she was desperate to have a child since she could not have her own and that's when she said I 'chose' her to be my mother. I didn't understand what that meant, and I certainly didn't understand her behavior at that moment.

"So, Michelle, Mom doesn't want you to live at home anymore." Dina explained.

"I don't understand why!" I blubbered.

"She believes your behavior is worse than it was and is not going to change." Dina was direct.

"Well, I haven't been home in over two months. I'm not quite sure how she thinks my behavior is worse, but I will work on that. By the way, I think I'm pregnant." I half-lied.

"We can confirm that through an appointment with Planned Parenthood, is that ok with you Lea?" Marie asked very calmly. I sat silent.

"I suppose so." Lea snapped. She would not even look at me. My plan seemed to be working. I was buying some extra time at home. I assumed at that point she realized she may have to keep me at home for a while and possibly have another mouth to feed.

"Lea, do you really want Michelle to leave now when this situation has come to light?" Marie asked.

"I don't know." Lea said very quietly.

"Why do you want her to leave so badly Lea?" Dina asked.

Lea sat quietly.

"Look, I'll do whatever she wants me to do as long as I don't have to leave." I begged.

"Ok, we'll get things set up for that appointment and once the results come in, we will go from there. Lea, are you ok with this?" Dina was concerned.

"I'll have to be, I suppose". Muttering under her breath. She looked so pissed off. It was as if nobody was validating her

76

feelings, and everyone was trying to protect me. She obviously didn't understand that.

"Mom, do you even love me?" I asked as the therapists waited for her answer holding their breath.

"I don't know, I suppose." She answered me. That was harsh but I expected nothing less.

As we waited in the office, one of the therapists made an appointment for me to go to Planned Parenthood within the next few days. Lea finally relented and agreed for me to stay as long as I did what I was told to do and to NEVER talk about my trip to Canada. Wow! As desperate as I was, I felt there was no choice. In hindsight, I probably should have run.

We arrived back home, and she made room enough for me to sleep on the cot in my old room. She would never remove all the boxes though. Lea would say I had enough room to sleep.

The next day, I finally went back to school. I was greeted by classmates and teachers asking about my trip. I told them all it was a good trip. Many were not aware of why I went to Canada, just that it was a summer trip with family. Needless to say, I left out all the problems I was having at home. Nobody needed to know that. I did not want any more interference.

A couple of days went by, school was boring, and I was distracted by so many things and thoughts. I was wondering if I actually was pregnant, as I was late. I had my appointment with Planned Parenthood that day. Lea drove me to that appointment. She was a ball of nerves and smoking non-stop like a chimney. We did not have much to say since our therapy session, so the last few days had been surprisingly quiet. While at Planned Parenthood, Lea decided to wait for me in the car. I went in and was met with a warm greeting and given a few pamphlets and a questionnaire to fill out. Ok. Done.

I was then taken into the back of the office where I was given a cup to pee in, and they would test it. I was led into another room where I would wait for a nurse to come in and give me a lecture about being a teenager having unprotected sex and what resources were out there for situations like mine if I was pregnant. The nurse asked me the typical questions about being a teenager, my social life, my home life, and on and on. All of which I answered as best as I could but not all answers were honest. My home life was "great." My social life was "ok." The nurse left the room for a moment and came back with the test result. I wasn't pregnant. Already, I knew that deep down. Now I had to go outside to tell Lea the news. I wasn't sure what would happen. I knew I was walking on eggshells.

As I was leaving the building, I could see Lea pacing outside in the driveway smoking a cigarette, looking very pale, tired and nervous. She saw me come out.

"Well?! Do I have to feed another mouth to feed?"
"No, I'm not pregnant" I stared at her face.

I never saw someone look so relieved but still so pissed off. She seemed to somehow know I was making it up. I braced for the consequences.

We got in the car and drove home in silence. She made soup and said we needed to get packed for the flea market on Sunday. It would be my first time back to the flea market that year.

"But it's only Thursday" I argued.
"We have a lot to pack up for" she retorted. "Don't argue with me."
"Ok, whatever." I shook my head.

I knew the rule for staying in the house was conditional on me doing *whatever* she said.

I began lifting the heavy boxes from the garage, bringing each one into the kitchen so Lea could quickly inspect them before I put them in the car. Lea wasn't kidding. There was a lot. I wasn't sure how we would pack everything into that damn station wagon, but we managed. I forgot how big that station wagon was. It took us a couple of days to pack it. Lea didn't work on it during the day because she didn't want to miss her TV shows or have to go to check on the apartments she owned.

Sunday finally came. We drove out to the flea market early that morning because she liked to get into her favorite spot due to the customers coming in droves to that particular area which was smart. We were unpacking and setting up the tables with her stuff. Pepper, as usual, was happily wagging her tail by my side. I was getting thirsty as the sun was rising high and I asked Lea for a couple of dollars to get something to drink. As she handed me the money, we saw her brother, Moe, and to our surprise, we saw Rita. They were setting up at the flea market too that day. Lea's mood turned from semi-good to crazed animal suddenly.

"If she comes over here, YOU WALK AWAY! Do you hear me?" She commanded. All of a sudden, she seemed so protective of me.

"Gladly!" I replied staunchly watching Rita who started to walk our way from three rows over. I really did not want to deal with Rita. I know she wanted to be nosy and ask questions about my trip and quite frankly, it was none of her business.
"She's headed this way now!" I cried.
"Go!" Lea demanded.

I walked away but not too far. I was curious to see and hear how Lea would react when Rita got to our space. Apparently, this was the first time Lea had seen Rita since the whole adoption bombshell happened back in April. I wasn't sure if Lea would ever forgive her sister-in-law for spilling the beans to me.

"Get away from us!" Lea screamed as Rita approached our space. Some people stopped in surprise and stared at her causing a scene.

"Lea, what's wrong?" Rita was acting as if she had no clue.

"Do you realize what you did to *my* daughter?!" Lea screamed at her vehemently.

I think she wanted to throw something at Rita. It wouldn't have surprised me. Lea couldn't stand Rita back then. I was also grappling with the fact that she finally said, *"my daughter."* Maybe, just maybe, there was some hope for her realizing how much all of this hurt me.

Rita walked away quietly and never came back. Although during the day, you could see her sitting on the tailgate of her husband's truck staring over our way. It was a long day, but I stayed put. I worked all day helping Lea out with the customers, wrapping up their newly found treasures to decorate their homes with and talking to other dealers who knew us. I always enjoyed the regular sellers and buyers at the flea market as many became like family. These flea market days were some of the few happy times in my childhood.

After that day, things were always up and down with Lea. She was angry, I was angry. There seemed to be no happy medium. I started skipping classes again and she got calls from the school. It got to the point where she would just unplug the phone. As for me, I just didn't know which way to turn anymore.

What made things even worse, Lea forced me to give up my precious chihuahua, Pepper. Lea never had her put down as she had threatened when I first came back. Despite Pepper always acting as my protector whenever Lea was raging, I knew it was time to protect her, so I went along with giving her a safe home away from our turmoil. I cried.

Pepper was the best dog for me. I adopted her from a lovely couple who came to the flea market often. They could not keep her as they had other animals. I would take Pepper everywhere I went. She was my little guardian fur angel. I would run into the couple who gave her to me from time to time and they were glad to see I was happy with her.

Lea would force me to give up a lot of pets over the years. Cats, dogs, and a couple of hamsters. She knew I loved them all, but she felt that I was paying too much attention to them. I do believe she was envious of my love for animals and their love for me but not for her. The only animal that mattered to her was her cat, Heather, that she had had for 16 years.

Being home from Canada was not easy at all. I was forced to get a job which was good but bad. I ended up working at a local Kentucky Fried Chicken which of course Lea thought I would be able to provide food besides just my paycheck. I couldn't bring home food every night, but I was able to take home what I could from time to time. Any money I made; Lea forced me to give her so she could pay her bills. If I asked for any of it, I would be denied. So, it went.

On my actual last night in her home sometime in November, Lea had picked a fight, she started coming after me with a lit cigarette and that damn leather strap. She got me in the arms with the lit cigarette and caught me in the torso and the face with the leather strap which caused several bruises. I cried, begged, and screamed at her to stop hurting me. I started to lunge back, pushing her away from me.

To be honest, I cannot remember what the fight was about. There were times she would just look at me and start to attack me physically and/or verbally. I would try to defend myself by holding up my arms and moving away from her. Afterwards, I remember from this particular night, she actually left the house, went to a neighbor's house to call the police in an effort to set me up. I heard the door open again and slam.

"Michelle! You need to come out here NOW" she yelled from down the hall.

"Why now?" I really didn't want to fight with her anymore. I was cleaning up my bruised and bloody nose. My hands were full of blood.

"A police officer is outside, and he wants to talk to you." She had this tone about her. Like she would win this time.

"For what? What did I do?"

"Just go outside for Christ's sake!" she pulled my arm and then pushed me violently towards the door.

I felt like I was detached from my body at this point. I walked outside. There was an officer standing in the driveway. He had wanted to come in to get me, but my mother of course would not let him come in. She was vehement that there was nothing to see in the house.

"Hi Michelle. I'm Officer Johnson. I'm here to help you and your mother." He was polite.

"I don't know why she called you!" I was sarcastic and hurting. It was dark as we stood on the front step. I think the light was too dim for him to really see any of the bruises I had.

"Your mother says you attacked her, and you are getting out of hand and wanted us to take you in." He explained.

"I NEVER attacked her. She attacked me! Look at me!" I had the red marks and dried blood on my face to prove she came after me. "I'm not out of hand. I only get upset when she starts to hit me." I explained.

He took out his flashlight and shined it on my face, he looked stern and wanted to question Lea.

"Lea, I'm sure things can calm down if you let Michelle calm down. She is a teenager, and these things happen. May I come into the house to look at any damage that may have been caused from the argument you had?" He again asked, this time a little more demanding.

"No! There's no need for you to come in and look at anything!" She spat.

Officer Johnson grew suspicious of Lea. He wanted to make sure I had what I needed and that I was safe. He knew I was hurt. At that time, there were no laws in place to assume Lea was the abuser. Today that would be a whole different story.

"If you don't take her away, I'm going to kill her tonight" her voice was venomous. She was serious.

"Please watch what you say. Michelle is just as upset as you are. Families usually work their problems out after a day or so. Can you just give this some time?" He tried to talk to her.

"Take her out of here, NOW!" She looked at me with such hate.

Officer Johnson looked at me rather frustrated and said "Michelle, why don't you go in and pack up some clothes for yourself for a few nights and I'll take you to the station to figure out a safe place for you."

"I give up...I'll pack some stuff." I threw up my arms.

"I don't want her in the house." She blocked my way.

"At least allow her to get some of her belongings," he pleaded. Lea felt cornered and relented.

I went into the house. I found a canvas bag to pack some stuff in for a few nights. The suitcase Sharon had given me had disappeared somewhere in the house. I was sure Lea had either hidden it or disposed of it.

I didn't have much clothing left since I had come home from Canada. I wore what I had and during my time back I didn't dare ask for anything. Lea didn't buy me anything for school so all I had was what I had brought home from Canada. I was lucky if I was given a notebook necessary for school.

Officer Johnson put me in the front seat of the cruiser, and he drove me to the station. He said he would have to call a social worker to pick me up and bring me to a local shelter for now. He was visibly upset at how Lea treated me and her behavior in general not letting him in to see the house. Honestly, if he had seen the inside, maybe something would have been done.

He had to type up a report. He asked me if I wanted medical attention for my injuries. He had to ask me questions about my relationship with my mother and told me to be honest. He knew I was afraid of getting her in trouble. As it was, the bruises I had from that night were becoming more noticeable on my face and arms. There were no laws in place at that time to arrest her, but the officer seemed adamant to hold her responsible. Triggered by the fact that she would not allow him in to see the condition of the house, he actually asked me if I wanted her arrested. I declined because I was very afraid of Lea at the time. Who wouldn't be?

After the officer typed his report, he called the hotline for the Department of Children and Youth Services to get a social worker to pick me up. I waited a while and I think it was almost midnight before the worker came in. During that time while I waited, I could see the officer talking to another officer and he paced back and forth. I knew he was probably thinking there had to be something he could do. It seemed obvious that I was being abused and neglected and I think he thought the house was probably deplorable. He would have been correct, but because I said no, his hands were tied.

Once again, I felt rejected and abandoned as the social worker came to transport me to a shelter for the time being.

CHAPTER 8 – LIVING IN FOSTER CARE

November 1985

The Salvation Army Shelter

I ended up staying at a shelter for a few weeks in the heart of Hartford and learned about street life in more ways than I could have imagined. It certainly wasn't in a good part of the city. As a vulnerable teenager, it was culture shock for me. I was scared. I couldn't sleep at night. I feared the unknown.

During the day, most of the shelter residents would hang out either out on the back porch or in the common room where they could visit with friends and family. There were no restrictions on time. Some of the younger residents went to the local high school and the adults went to jobs or learned job skills. I didn't attend school while waiting for a foster home. I felt as I was in limbo. Meals were prepared and served at set times by the volunteers that came in. The curfew for bedtime or lights out was usually around 10:00 p.m. I remember one night before curfew; I was sitting outside on the back porch with a few of the residents. I didn't do much, still not feeling comfortable with these people. That particular night, a Hispanic-looking man carrying a baseball bat walked into the parking lot by the porch and started talking to a couple of the male residents. He obviously knew some of them. He was wearing a red bandana and red shirt. I was unaware at the time that these were gang colors. His eyes suddenly locked on mine. I saw that he had an unusual tear drop tattoo by his right eye. I felt uncomfortable and quickly went back inside. I never went back outside again at night while at shelter.

Despite many calls with DCF, a social worker told me that Lea would never answer the phone.

I went into the shelter's office to ask if I could use the residential phone to call Lea and was told I could use it anytime. I picked up the receiver and my fingers shook. Why was I calling her?!

"Hello?" Lea answered quietly.

"Mom?" I asked.

"What do you want?" She was annoyed.

"It's scary here at the Shelter," I said.

"So?" Now she was being sarcastic.

"There are roaches all over the bedrooms and in the shower," I sobbed, then started to explain to her that there were some shifty people lurking around the parking lot late at night.

"Well, you deserve to be there. Whatever happens now is on you!" She yelled.

"Mom, you really hurt me the other night. I hope you know that. The bruises I have hurt, especially on my face." I was trying to get through to her that I wanted to start over and go home.

"Oh...so sorry about that!" She was so loathing.

"I don't know where they're going to send me, do you?" I pleaded.

"No and I don't care." She seemed to be deadly quiet at this point.

"Well, if I go to a home near you, can I stop by to get my clothes and things?" I begged.

"Oh sure!" I didn't realize it then, but it was yet another sarcastic answer. It felt like she was mocking me at this point.

"I'll call you when there is news on the placement, ok?" I didn't know what else to say. I knew deep down, I was never going back to her house to live.

"Go to hell!" Were her last words to me as she slammed the phone down, without ever saying good-bye.

I soon realized that I actually was going into the foster care system. DCF began looking for a foster home to take me in. This time, it was real, and I could do nothing about it. In retrospect, years later I would realize this shelter was a dream compared to living in Lea's house.

During the following days, I waited to hear back from George, the state social worker for DCF regarding a possible foster home in my hometown. I had told George that I would run away if they couldn't find me something there. I just wanted to be in familiar surroundings and get back to school. He was trying but I was not making it easy on him with my daily pleas. My mind was swirling with all the core memories of the abuse I had suffered because of Lea. Despite the past year of me skipping a lot of school, I missed going to school now.

I missed Canada. My life as I knew it was at a standstill. No school, no real friends, no family.

And while I waited, I called Lea again one night, knowing that would be the only time to catch her. I asked her if I could please stop by the house with the social worker to get some of my clothes in case a foster placement opened up for me. She had agreed and I wanted to believe her. Instead, she packed the suitcase Sharon gave me with whatever I had left and brought it to DCF herself. She obviously did not want me coming by the house under any circumstances.

First Home

Just before Thanksgiving, George found a foster home in my town that had a spare bed. George picked me up and brought me there the next afternoon. I met the foster mother and her oldest daughter who recognized me from school. She looked familiar to me, but I didn't really know her. They both seemed nice. That evening I met the rest of the family when I sat with them quietly at the dinner table. I looked around at the clean home and stared at the family in deep thought. I wondered if this is what a real family looked like. I shared my room with the family's youngest daughter, about five years younger than me, with a bunk bed. I slept on the bottom of a bunk bed. The room was tiny with floral wallpaper and a few scattered stuffed animals. For the moment, I appreciated having a warm bed and a roof over my head. There was also another foster child about my age, who stayed in the room next to mine. The house itself felt a bit cramped. It didn't take me long to realize wherever this family had extra room, they rented it for extra money. The back of garage, the attic, and even a portion their den was occupied by grown men who needed a place to live. It was more like a boarding house than a home. We all shared one bathroom which struck me as being a bit weird since there were teen girls in the same house. Regardless, the family always had first dibs on use of the bathroom.

During the first few weeks, I really kept to myself. It appeared they did not have either of their foster kids' interests at heart. It wasn't long before I learned what this family was really all about. Money. I felt very lonely and out of place.

At the start of December, I called Lea asking if I could come home for Christmas and she said no. I asked her if she would come visit me. She said had to think about things, but she would never come. As time went on, I learned that this foster mother had called the new social worker assigned to my case asking for more money for their electricity bill because I was staying in more often than house more than others which was not true.

I became very close with the foster teen, Peg, who also lived in the house. (We are still close friends today) While we hung out in different social circles, we still bonded. She became pregnant while living there and I was the only one who knew about it.

While Peg and I stayed in that home, we had few restrictions. We were free to roam the streets around town and hang out with whoever. Although, it was made clear to us that if we weren't home by dinnertime, we would not eat. If we were not back by curfew at 10:00 P.M., we were left outside. I got to know some of the neighborhood residents albeit some more questionable than others. After the initial weeks of keeping to ourselves inside the home, Peg and I started spending more time out of the house except to sleep at night.

To my delight, I discovered that the family that adopted my dog Pepper didn't live too far from me and that I was able to visit her on occasion. The first time Pepper saw me and realized who I was, she went crazy with exciting couldn't stop kissing my face. It brought tears to my eyes. These moments between a girl and her dog would be the only unconditional love I ever felt as a child. Pepper was a blessing to me as I adjusted to my new life as a foster child.

Peg and I had several run-ins with the foster family kids. Both of us survived several incidents in the foster home with their son attempting to take advantage of us while we lived there. One night Peg had an argument with the fosters' oldest daughter which quickly turned into a physical altercation. Apparently, the daughter had stolen some clothes from Peg. Peg confronted her and all went south from there. They argued and fought until the police were called.

Peg ended up having to leave the house but not without getting very upset and trying to hurt herself by banging her head on a wall with frustration. I went in to calm her down. I knew she was pregnant, but the foster parents were unaware. I didn't want her to have any issues with her pregnancy, so I stood between her and the wall. She was moved out of the home that night. To this day, although we had lost a few years growing up, we never lost our bond. We were in the same position as foster kids, which created a closeness I hated to lose, but we were eventually separated. Growing up without her, I often thought back to my friend Peg and wondered how she was doing. I learned through my social worker that she had the baby and was living with the father's family somewhere in town.

After Peg moved out, I moved into her bedroom but never felt safe in that house. There were times I would literally have to lock my door when their son was home. I didn't trust him or the other random men who lived there. I complained about the home to the social worker but was told point blank by the head of the agency that they would just hold off sending other girls to them for 'a while.'

That summer I was able to go back to Canada to visit with my birth family again. Although it was only for a week, it was a nice respite for me. From a part-time job at a supermarket, I was able to pay back my grandmother for the phone bill I had run up the summer before. I seem to have proven to them that I was honorable. Even my brother was back home so we finally had a chance for some sibling bonding albeit too short. It was sad to leave them again but felt assured that it would not be my last time at the reservation.

Back in Connecticut, over the next few months, I continued going to school (most of the time) and working my part time job at the store. I always walked to my job as the family wouldn't provide transportation to the store which was a couple of miles away. I wanted some money of my own, but it was never enough. I liked working at the supermarket. I got to know the family who owned it and I liked our produce manager, Roger, who was good for a few laughs. He was a gentle soul. We began a friendship at the store. He and his wife, Connie, were older and had several grown children. They became like pseudo-parents to me, integral to my needs at the time.

From spending so much time walking to and from my job plus hanging out with some questionable friends at school, I learned a little more about street life. I was turned on to alcohol frequently. I used an illicit drug here and there. I thought it was the thing to do at the time and, quite frankly, I did it out of boredom. I was sad. I felt alone.

As time went on in the foster home, I began spending more and more time at work. Because my job was only part time and I did not have much of a social life, I tried to take as many work hours after school as possible. I found out that Lea was calling the foster home to see what I was up to and my foster mother would fill her in. By that point, my relationship with my mother was estranged and I had stopped calling her. My opinion was that my life was none of her business anymore. Since she didn't want me, why should she care? But I was also suspicious of Lea. I was sure she was looking for something to set me up with. I wouldn't be wrong. I had really changed my attitude towards her. I told my foster mother that I didn't want her talking to Lea and she laughed in my face. Privacy laws were not in place at the time. I complained to my social worker who agreed with me but unfortunately, there was nothing they could do. I stayed in this home for about ten months total. That was enough of this family. I was asked by my social worker if I wanted to move back to Canada. I said no. I explained that a nice couple from work offered me the opportunity to move in with them. I decided to move in with Roger and Connie, a couple who genuinely cared. There would be no state involvement unless it became necessary, and Lea would not know where I was.

Second Home

From the moment I met Roger and Connie, they were so nice to me. They genuinely took an interest in me and where I came from. They knew I was a foster kid living in a dysfunctional home. After hearing my story, Roger knew I wanted to get out of there as we often talked about things. He had told me that he and his wife wanted to take in a foster child. I didn't realize at the time they were opening their hearts to me. One night at the store about closing time, I saw Roger walk in. I was surprised to see him. I was counting my cash register money at the end of my shift for the night and before I had to walk back to the foster home.

"Hey Michelle, do you want to come to our house for strawberry shortcake with me and Connie? I can give you a lift back to your home afterward."

"Sure!" I must have sounded elated to be invited over.

I had to call my foster home and say that I was going to be a little late and asked that they please not lock the door. They took it into consideration and didn't lock the door for the first time. It was the only time that I would have ever been late.

We closed the store and went on our way. I got into Roger's car, and he drove me to his home. Along the way, he was very nice, and told me about his house, his family and his wife.

They lived in a beautiful small ranch house which was set along a scenic wooded area with a walking path towards a large fishing pond in the back. The moment I walked into their home, it smelled like cinnamon and was impeccably clean. I felt warm and comfortable. Is this what a real home feels like?

During a round of strawberry shortcake, they asked me if I'd like to live with them. I didn't say yes right away. I would need to talk about it with my social worker first. They understood and offered to go with me to talk to her. I said I would let them know. The next day I spoke with my social worker who seemed elated for me. Roger and Connie's home was not officially a foster home but the idea of moving in with them was a good one. They seemed kind and I trusted them. My social worker set it up so that I would be on the state's independent program for older foster kids, and I would be on their assistance program for the duration until I was 21, as long as I stayed in school. I was thrilled at the thought! I was going to be free. Well, sort of free.

My impending plans would not be without problems from Lea. She had heard from my foster mother that I was moving out. The foster mother was not given any information as to where I was moving to. I had made a stance with DCF that no information be given out. They held to their promise. I felt I had to call Lea one afternoon because for some reason she had come looking for me to find out where I was going.

"Hello?" She answered.

"Mom?" I said.

"What do you want?" Funny, I thought she would be kinder.

"I heard you want to know where I am going." I began.

"That's right. Where are you going? I have a right to know," she retorted.

"No, you have no rights to me anymore." I hung up the phone.

I went to the store that night to start my shift but all the while I would be thinking about our phone conversation so much so that I would call her back on a break.

"Hello?" She answered.

"Stay out of my life." I was calm and hung up the phone.

I felt vindicated but also guilty. I shouldn't have felt guilty. She was absolutely up to something, but I wouldn't worry about this yet. Over the next couple of weeks, as I prepared for my move out of the foster home, I received a call from my social worker asking me to come down to her office that afternoon. I was surprised to receive that call but maybe it had to do with my paperwork for the assistance program. I didn't know.

As I reached the DCF office just down the road from the foster home, I waited in the lobby for my social worker. She came and brought me into their conference room and sat me down.

"Michelle, your mother came to see me," she explained. I shook my head and wondered what now?

"For what?" I asked.

"She is accusing you of stealing $500.00 out of her purse when she wasn't looking." She further explained. I was in shock. Seriously?

"Well, I certainly haven't stolen from her and how could I? I never see her. You know this." I was gut punched again.

"Michelle, I want to believe you...." She would go on...

"Then BELIEVE me! I'm so sick of her doing this to me!" I yelled.

"Let's call her on the phone and talk to her through the speaker, ok?" She suggested.

"That's fine. Let's!" I commanded.

As the phone rang, I was ready to throw the phone through the window. I hated Lea at that moment. She knew I was moving. She had no idea where I was going, and she couldn't stand it! She knew she had no more control over me.

"Hello?" Lea answered.

"Mom, how dare you!" I exclaimed.

"How dare I what?" She yelled.

"You accused me of stealing $500 out of your purse! You know I didn't steal any money from you! I haven't been with you, nor have I been to your house in months!" I confronted her.

"Yes, you did. I had money in my purse, and you came over and stole it," she accused me.

"Funny mom, I don't even have a key to the house."

"Well, I know you did it. I want it back."

"Um, I can't give back what I didn't take. You know you're on speakerphone with me and my social worker, right?" I replied.

She immediately hung up the phone. My social worker apologized to me and continued to set me up for the independent living program. The social worker would have a phone conversation later with Lea telling her that she believed me. Lea couldn't stand it. The game was over.

It was such a breath of fresh air to move in with Roger and Connie. I moved in with them in August of 1986. Their grown kids came over to help me get settled in. It was a good move. Everyone in that family was supportive. I became close to all of them, especially their daughters who were adults and had their own families. They all had a bond that I ached for, but my wall was high and nearly impossible to break down.

Unfortunately, my family fantasy would be short lived. My stay there lasted only lasted about six weeks. I had gotten into some trouble with the police while living there after spending some money I found at work that wasn't mine. This would have nothing to do with Lea and her accusations because I never stole from her. This was something I did stupidly on my own. I lost my job at the job at the store …and I lost my home with Roger and Connie.

It became a very misguided opinion that I was going to embarrass the family (which never happened) and Roger and Connie felt it best that I leave. The trust was broken. I was still grateful to Roger and Connie for the chance they gave me, but I knew that leaving was for the best. I was immediately sent to a state-run group home for at risk girls for structure and guidance otherwise I would have been thrown into a juvenile detention center (or worse) like my brother Mike was. The choice was obvious. I heard the worst stories about detention centers. I didn't want to go there or anywhere else.

The Third Home

I moved into a state-run group home a few towns over for approximately one and a half years. The other resident girls would come and go, dependent on their placement. Some would come for a few days; others would stay for years until they aged out of the foster system at 21. The home was clean. The staff was consistent and most of the time good with us. I bonded with much of the staff. The home was tightly run by a former nun, Jean. Jean could be scary at times. I was able to go to a different high school that was much smaller where nobody knew me. That was a welcome relief. There was no bullying in the last two years of high school, and I was finally able to make several good friends. The group home was different. We would antagonize each other, and we would fight but, in the end, it would calm down and we would go on about our structured day, of getting up, eating breakfast, going to school, come home, do our homework, chores next, and then, it was quiet time before bed. We did not refuse to do anything we were told because we would either be grounded, or Jean would come at us verbally. If she was feeling especially mean spirited, she would have one of her dogs intimidate us if she felt we were out of line. I remember one time she had instigated by pushing me 'unintentionally' and her dog, Beau jumped up on me and just growled. Jean thought it was funny. Jean also liked to talk about our cases and situations with other parents who would call for an update on their own daughters. These parents got more than they bargained for with Jean.

Today, that would have been cause for legal problems concerning privacy. Whenever I think of Jean, I still quiver a bit. She was who she was, and we had to have thick skin around her. I thought I had tough skin; it just wasn't tough enough sometimes.

Jean was rough on the staff too. The staff never took it out on us though. They were good to me and the other girls and today, I still have a relationship with some of the girls I lived with during that time. My stay at this group home offered me the first opportunity to form true friendships with my roommates. We bonded together because, despite our circumstances, we only had each other to lean on.

Sometimes we went on weekend trips with some of the staff. One trip we went to Niagara Falls. Imagine eight girls and two staff members in one big van. That was a memorable and long trip. I remember swimming in the indoor pool at the hotels we stayed at, having local meals, and going to the falls on either side of the border. We were given a small stipend to spend on souvenirs if we wanted to. All in all, it was a nice experience. Aside from my trips to see my birth family in Canada, I had never gone on any vacation in my life.

My New Foster Parents Geoff and Elaine

One day back at the group home, my social worker, Ingrid, visited me and told me she wanted me to meet a British couple who lived nearby. Geoff and Elaine were foster parents specifically focused on taking in Native American children. They had already adopted four Native American children. They were interested in taking me in and adopting me but were told that I was 'too old' to be adopted. However, after meeting them, I became very fortunate to have found the seemingly perfect foster parents, who were able to stand by me and bring me back to my roots. While I did not live with them full time, they did all they could for me on weekends, during school vacations and summers. They often drove many miles to pick me up and bring me to their home or to Native American cultural events. They knew what I needed. I needed them.

Geoff and Elaine were the co-founders of the Connecticut River Powwow Society and hosted yearly powwows to educate the public about Native Americans. These events would bring thousands of natives from all over the Western Hemisphere including Zuni and Aztec dancers, some famous Native Americans like Floyd Redcrow Westerman, a folk singer, and a pretty well-known tv/film actor. Getting to know Floyd was special to me as he opened my mind to the spiritual world and the spiritual animals that are always guiding us. Although I was young, from that moment on, I began to understand the importance of the connection between clans, totems, spirit animals, and our ancestors. The Mohawks used a clan system consisting of three ruling spirit animals, Bear, Turtle and Wolf. I was adopted into the Turtle clan (symbolic for peace) but was originally born into the Bear clan (symbolic for strength). Mother earth brings us all together.

At these native powwow events, I was mesmerized watching my people dance and sing in their regalia (animals skins feathered headdresses, and beaded jewelry). They stomped in circles to the beat of a drum. I felt moved by Spirit to join. I came to the event already dressed in native garb, so it felt natural to begin dancing with my native people. I believe this is when I started my own healing journey. I remember these

97

powwows were beautiful events. I felt at home, surrounded by *my* people. And although Geoff and Elaine were British, they were revered by many native nations. It was a priceless time in my young life. They gave me a part of myself back through everyone that participated in these events. Geoff and Elaine have become a forever part of my life and in all honesty, became like parents to me through thick, thin, good and bad.

The Death of my grandmother, Mary – Part 1

While in the group home, I received letters from both Sharon and my grandmother telling me how the family was doing and who was doing what. My grandmother would write to me more often and send me American money for things I needed at the time. She would tell me how much she loved and missed me and only wished the best for me.

I remember two specific letters from her. To this day, I have held onto these letters as they mean so much to me. As I reread them from time to time, I feel the tears well up in my eyes and my heart begins to break all over again.

In one letter, she admitted she knew I ached to meet my biological father. Both she and Sharon knew I longed to put a face to the man that helped create me. My grandmother wrote that she didn't want me to find my biological father as she didn't want me to get hurt again. She became fiercely protective of me.

In her last letter to me, Grandma explained that she had become sick. She was diagnosed with Non-Hodgkin's Lymphoma. I am not sure what stage she was at the time, but I think when she was diagnosed, it was too late. She tried to assure me that there was nothing to worry about but as little as I knew about this kind of cancer, I knew it wasn't good.

I would write to my grandmother some more, but I only received one last Christmas card from her with $100 in American money. She wanted me to buy something nice for myself. That would be the last correspondence I would receive.

The Fourth Home

At the end of my stay, I left that state-run group home on unsavory terms because of Jean. I was not able to take any more verbal abuse and I was ready for independence and was in search of an alternative place to live. I was eighteen when I left that home to go to another group home. Although I had to leave my friends and finish my senior year at yet another high school, it was a much better fit for me as it was more of an independent living program.

The Death of my grandmother, Mary - Part 2

As I settled into this new independent living group home, in March, 1988, I received a call from Sharon who said that Grandma was in the hospital and had been asking for me. I had just started at the new high school, so I wasn't able to go to Canada until April vacation. Over the next three weeks, that was all I could think about. The quarterly stipend I received from DCF immediately went to buy my round-trip ticket.

When I finally got to Montreal, Sharon picked me up and drove me back to my grandmother's house to sleep. Sharon still lived here, as well. My grandmother was still in the hospital. I slept in her bed at home. I remember it was one of the only times I felt completely safe and at peace.

The next morning, we went to the hospital so I could visit with her. As I walked into her room, I could see she had lost all her hair from the radiation treatment she received. She had a large tumor on the left side of her face. It was very traumatic to see her like this. She was not able to eat a lot. She lost a significant amount of weight. She went from a woman with curly white hair to being bald within the two years I knew her.

Grandma held her arms out to me when I stepped into her hospital room, and we quickly embraced for a long bear hug. The room, like the hospital, was cold and sterile. Grandma loved the company that would come to visit her. She would ask about school and if I was settling into the new home well. I explained that I was doing fine. Didn't need to worry her about anything. I just wanted to see her get better so I could have a little more time with her.

I spent the next few days going back and forth from her house to the hospital. It was important and Sharon would tell me that Grandma did nothing but ask for me. I believe she knew her time was coming.

"My dear, I'm sorry you have to see me like this." Grandma said, quietly.

"Grandma, you'll get better and be back to yourself soon." I lied but prayed that maybe I was telling the truth.

"I don't know about that," she replied.

"Sure, you will." I pushed, trying to hold back my tears.

"Do you forgive me dear?" Grandma asked honestly. She wanted to be forgiven for forcing Sharon to give me up.

"Grandma, there's nothing to forgive. You did what you thought was right!" I held her arm and kissed her cheek.

"You have no idea how much better that makes me feel." She cried holding her arms out to me. I lied on the hospital bed with her and hugged her for what seemed like forever. She really did feel guilty about forcing Sharon to give me up. There was no question, I forgave her.

"I don't know how much longer I'll be here, but I hope I see you again soon." I didn't realize it at that moment, but she was talking about her death. She realized she didn't have much time left. I was torn having to go back to Connecticut the next morning.

"I promise to come back this summer, ok?" I assured her. She nodded.

"Ok honey, just know that I love you dearly." She hugged me again, so tightly. I loved her.

As I left that morning to get on the Greyhound bus, I had an overwhelming feeling come over me that this would be the last time I would see my grandmother alive, but I suppressed it. I was in denial.

About two weeks later as I was coming back to the group home from school, my DCF social worker was there to pay me a visit. She was called by the director of the home informing her that my grandmother had passed away that morning. I honestly thought the social worker was there for a social visit to see how things were going, not to deliver the blow that knocked my sails out.

"Hi Michelle, the home received a call that your grandmother passed away this morning." She told me sympathetically.

"What? No, that's wrong. I just talked with her on the phone a few days ago!" I cried, almost hysterical.

"I'm afraid it's not wrong. Your grandmother did pass away. Your mother, Lea, will take you to the bus station in the morning. The wake will be held for two days, and the funeral will be held Friday." She even sounded surprised that Lea would somehow find her way back into my life for this event.

Despite a small sprinkling of Lea sightings over the past two years while I lived at the group homes, she had been pretty absent from my life at the time.

In tears, I excused myself to go to my room to once again pack for a trip to Canada the next morning. It was surreal that I was going out of the country 2 times in one month. I was in a fog losing my grandmother. Grandma was a huge influence in my life, even if for a short while. She told me things and tried to teach me things. Her letters to me were priceless as I felt I wasn't so alone in the predicament I was in. Her voice is what I heard and felt in my heart.

The next day, I found myself dreading getting back on that Greyhound bus. Lea drove me to the bus station, telling me that she was sorry about my grandmother, and I'll feel better saying goodbye to her. I was surprised at Lea's warmth over the situation.

As I made my way onto the bus, it felt cold and dark. I didn't even look out the window to see if Lea was still there, perhaps to wave me off but my intuition told me she wasn't. I just wasn't feeling the trip and I snoozed for most of the ride. Maybe because I was going to a funeral this time around. Maybe I was in denial that my grandmother was dead. I didn't know what to expect at a Native American funeral. When I arrived in Montreal, my brother Mike and a family friend were at the bus station waiting to pick me up. Mike asked if I was in a hurry to get back to the house and I told him I was. I just wanted to get cleaned up and changed. He was disappointed because he had noticed a gentlemen's club across the street from the bus station and he and his friend wanted to go there for a drink before heading back. *Seriously Mike?!* I was appalled, but my brother appeased me and brought me back to the house. I wouldn't see him again until the next day's calling hours at the funeral home. I knew I had to back down on my frustration with him because I figured he was hurting too. Mike and our grandmother were very close.

As I showered and changed into fresh clothes to go to the wake that night, I heard a loud knock on the door. I was alone in the house and a bit nervous to open the door. I heard a loud male voice.

"Sharon!" the man yelled in a thick French accent.
"Sharon are you in there?" He would yell again.
"Sharon isn't here." I yelled back, hoping this guy would go away!
"Can I come in?" He pleaded.
"Sharon isn't here. Come back another time please." The door opened. I had left it unlocked in case Sharon or my brother came back while I was getting ready.

I stood behind my grandmother's kitchen chair watching this tall strange dark-haired man coming up the steps from the side door. I was in a 'protect myself mode' ready to hurl the kitchen chair and whatever else I could at him.

"Sharon here?" He asked again.

"No. She's not. I think she's at the funeral home." I explained, holding tightly to the chair.

"Who are you?" He asked. I wasn't sure if I should answer him.

"I'm Michelle, Sharon's daughter," I announced.

"What?" He turned pale and looked stunned. Did he not hear me correctly?

"Michelle, Sharon's daughter?" I said, again.

"Oh my God! I'm Serge, Mike's father!" He looked bewildered.

"Are you, my daughter?" He started to interrogate me.

"Nope, I belong to someone named Ed." I was honest.

"Oh well, wow! You scared me!" He said.

"And you scared me." I stared at him.

"I'm going to leave, please tell Sharon I stopped by." Oh don't worry. I will.

About an hour later, Sharon came home to take me to the funeral home where my beautiful grandmother would be laid out. Sharon went to get a beer in the fridge when I told her about the visitor.

"Sharon, you'll never guess who stopped by." I was a little hesitant to tell her.

"Who?" She wasn't expecting anyone.

"Serge? Mike's father?" I said, waiting for her response.

"WHAT?!" She was dumbfounded nearly dropping her beer bottle. She couldn't believe he had shown up.

"Yea, he just opened the door and in he came. He scared me to be honest." I told her.

103

Sharon nearly spit out the sip of beer she had just taken. She looked as if she had seen a ghost. Apparently, she hadn't seen Serge for many years and for him to just show up was beyond her. That was the first and last time I ever saw Serge. He never did come back to see Sharon, that I know of.

As I arrived at the funeral home that night, it was a warm and inviting sanctuary. My grandmother was laid out beautifully in a white casket with pink rose inlays on each corner. There were lots of people just hanging out on the enclosed porch and many inside just sitting in silence as is expected in Mohawk tradition. Many knew me, others were just meeting me for the first time. The wake would last for two days and two nights. The doors were open 24 hours a day. People would sometimes go at 2:00 in the morning, while others like the family would go during the day and early at night. It was a traditional custom for people to stay with the body until the funeral. I stayed there both days for a few hours just thinking about my grandmother, how much time I lost with her, and how I wished she were still with us.

The day arrived to say our final goodbye and the funeral procession was about to begin. We all lined up to kiss my grandmother goodbye. Sharon and her five siblings, me, my brother and the rest of my cousins, Mary's grandchildren. All of Mary's grandchildren placed their photographs in her casket to be buried with her.

My brother became very emotional when it came his turn to say goodbye. It was difficult to console him as he pushed people away. My grandmother, in many ways, was like his mother than Sharon was at the time. Remember, Sharon had been a teen mom, so Mary had assumed much of the parental role. Mike loved our grandmother so much. I couldn't begin to imagine his anguish, never mind comprehending feeling my own anguish for a woman that I only had for two years of my life. The ceremony was a simple Catholic mass ceremony on the reservation. The same Church I was baptized in eighteen years earlier. After the service, we escorted the hearse to the cemetery where we circled around the gravesite hearing the birds above, listening to the prayers being said, a couple of women chanted a long prayer in Mohawk. A light rain began to fall. It was thought to be tears from our Mohawk ancestors. The Catholic priest said his final prayer and we, her family, grabbed some dirt and threw it on top of the casket as it settled into the ground. That day was surreal to me. I was never going to see my grandmother again. I was reminded by the community of our Mohawk spirit animal, the Bear, which would continue to protect us. It brought me some comfort.

Back at my grandmother's house, we had a huge lunch which included food given by many friends and family members. I was introduced to two of my grandmother's sisters and some other cousins that lived close by. I heard Sharon talking to some people in my grandmother's bedroom. I went into the room and sat on my grandmother's bed listening to happy stories about my grandmother being told. I suddenly felt tired, and I lied down on her bed, trying to keep my eyes open but I couldn't fight the exhaustion. As I put my head down on my grandmother's pillow, I remember hearing someone say, just as I was falling asleep "I couldn't sleep in a dead person's bed!" I could. I felt warm and safe in my grandmother's bed.

The next day, I traveled by bus back to Connecticut. I was in such a fog after the funeral that I barely remembered the trip home. The fog was thick.

When I settled back into the group home, I was quiet. I felt a new sense of responsibility toward myself and my future. Death taught me that we are not immortal beings on this earth. Life had to go on, but it wasn't easy. I trusted my spirit animal, Bear, was with me.

This home I was now living in was somewhat similar to the first state-run group home but different in some ways. We had to be in school, work, and study and live as if we were on our own. We were taught to cook, clean, dress appropriately, and take care of our own finances. It was a small group of girls in this home, and we formed close friendships, some that would come full circle many years later in our adult lives. I'll never forget the bond we shared then and the bonds that I share today with Kim B (who passed at age 41), Bleighne, Kim H., Kim W., Jenn, Annie, and Nita. We were and are everything to each other, today, though we might be miles apart in some cases, we always know how to find each other.

The program at this group home went well and about a year and a half later, I was ready to finally be free and totally independent. However, there were lessons to be learned once I finally was on my own.

And so, I went...

CHAPTER 9 – BREAKING FREE

My younger years through high school were spent bouncing between relatives' homes, in and out of Lea's house, my native reservation in Canada, a salvation army shelter, foster families and group homes. I ended up attending three different high schools. Crazy times, but I somehow made it through.

September1989

Transitioning Into My Own Home

At 19, I knew it was time to get myself out of the foster care system and go out on my own. I was more than ready, and I was desperate to live by myself for a while without a roommate, although in hindsight, I should have had a roommate to help with expenses. I had the opportunity to stay in my last group home until I was 21 but I honestly had had enough. I was fiercely independent and thought I had it all figured out. Ha! I probably should have stayed in the last home a little while longer.

I certainly learned about responsibility and independence. Sometimes independence isn't all that it's supposed to be when you're young. I also learned about relationships in the real world. Some were good, some were bad, some were ok.

Surprisingly, I kept in touch with Lea on occasion. Lea and I were on somewhat better, but still rocky terms. She was there for me off and on as she felt like it. I think on some level she knew she was responsible for a lot of what happened and decided to help me in her own way as I began my transition to independence.

Since I didn't have a car at the time, she became my transportation on Saturdays for grocery shopping. Otherwise, I would walk to work and other places I needed to go. Many times, I would have friends and coworkers pick me up for work and drop me off after work. I made do, and it was what it was.

I was ok by myself for about a year but ended up almost homeless when the eviction process loomed at the apartment I was living in. I had very limited finances. It was clear I needed a roommate to help with expenses. Luckily, I found a new close friend, Ellen, at my new job. We worked together as cashiers at a local retail store and spent evenings socializing at a nearby bar. She also worked as a police dispatcher in town. She was a single mom with a teenage son, and they welcomed me into their home. Shortly after moving in, we rented a larger apartment in the same building. I could barely afford the rent but did what I could with what I had. There were months I came up short, but Ellen was good to me taking it all in stride. She knew I had a lot on my plate aside from a full-time job, I had also started classes at the local community college. Ellen was like a mother to me. Our bond of friendship was strong.

While living with Ellen in this apartment complex, it would ultimately be the place where I would meet my future husband, Mike.

February 1991

Meeting My Husband

I met Mike in February 1991. He was 34 and I was 21. Let me back up. I actually met Mike before our 'first meeting'. He was the superintendent of our apartment complex. We would run into each other on various occasions/different times in the building lobby, hallways, or laundry room. We would sometimes trade general pleasantries, or he would make a joke to make me giggle like any 21-year-old college girl.

On a cold morning in February, as I was leaving the apartment for school, I stepped onto the elevator, felt it shake and come to a sudden stop. I was jolted. I could hear voices, so I knocked on the walls.

"Hello?!" I yelled out.

"Are you stuck in the elevator?" I heard someone ask.

"Yes, I am." I was not a fan of small spaces.

Within minutes, Mike came to my rescue. My hero. He was able to get the doors open. When he saw me, he started to make a funny crack.

"I think I see you more than 'the' wife". He laughed. Damn, I thought. He's married. He's cute too. Oh well, on my way to my day I went.

"Oh really? You're a funny guy!" Awkward!

The next morning, I ran into Mike coming down my hallway. I thanked him again for 'rescuing' me the day before and he remarked "think nothing of it."

"Hey, would you like to come over to my place for some wine coolers?" He asked.

I must have looked at him like he had two heads. I was confused by his question.

"Sure, what about your wife?" I asked coyly.

It was his turn to look at me like I had two heads. Now it appeared like he was confused.

"What do you mean? I don't have a wife. What made you think I did?"

Hmmm, did I hear him wrong yesterday? I felt a little jittery. The hairs on the back of my neck stood up giving me cause to think 'Ok buddy – what'd you do with your wife in the last 24 hours?'

"Didn't you tell me you see me more than 'the wife?' I was serious. He started to laugh pretty hard.

"No. No. No. You misheard me. I said I see you more than 'A' wife." He chuckled again.

Well…egg on my face. I must've had selective hearing. I probably should have gotten my ears checked.

I looked at him sheepishly "Well then, sure. I'd love to come over for some wine coolers, but I have class until 9:30 p.m. – would that be ok?

"Of course, I'll see you then. Call me if anything should change, ok?". He wrote down his number and I took it.
"Will do."

So off I went thinking about what just happened. I remember smiling wide yet feeling like an idiot for misinterpreting his words.

The next night was the night. I was looking forward to sharing that cold wine cooler with Mike. I went to my class but could barely pay attention. I was thankful we were let out early. I got home, freshened up and changed quickly. I was at Mike's door a half-hour early, in one of the apartment buildings adjacent to mine. I knocked and he answered the door smiling.

"Hope you don't mind, the professor let us out early". I smiled.
"Not at all, please come in." He opened the door wider.

I noticed a beautiful apartment with lots of closet space and 14-foot-high ceilings. It was so different from my apartment despite being in the same complex. I didn't realize each apartment floor was unique. Mike's apartment had an amazing layout and that was just the first floor. I hadn't seen the second floor but noticed a loft above the living room. It was beautiful. He obviously had great domestic ability.

As we sat, he gave me a choice of which wine cooler I would enjoy, and he had one himself. He sat down on one end of the beautiful sectional, and I sat sort of in the middle. It was a cozy dim lit atmosphere. He had some light 70's rock music playing in the background. We began talking about life. He was a generation older than me. We had quite the age gap, but it didn't matter. I always liked older men. He said he had been divorced for about five years and was just coming out of a relationship where he was engaged to an opera singer, but it just did not work out. The more he talked the more I noticed how handsome and rugged he was. He talked about his job and what he looked forward to in life. He didn't have a lot of money but that didn't bother me. He seemed to be an honest, hard worker. I had an immediate respect for him.

As we talked, something above us had caught my attention and I looked up to make sure I was seeing what I saw correctly. Sure enough, it was a beautiful black cat peeking out from over the loft railing. Her name was Keesha. She was very curious but didn't come down, although Mike had said she had jumped down from the loft before and I kind of hoped she wouldn't do that. She didn't. She was a quiet girl just checking me out. Mike explained how he had adopted Keesha as a very tiny kitten who was lost in the woods and had to be bottle fed. She was just his pride and joy, and you could tell she adored him. It was a great way to end the evening. The cat wasn't our only interruption that night, though. We had a nice evening of wine coolers and talking, but with the couple next door moaning and groaning very loudly, it was obvious what they were doing. I think that was my cue to leave. I realized I needed to get back to my apartment and crack the books for an exam in the morning.

"Wow, it's getting late, and I have classes tomorrow." I was tired. He understood.

"Oh ok, I really enjoyed tonight. It's been a long time since I had the pleasure of talking with someone as nice as you". He smiled at me. We gave each other a kiss on the cheek, and we said goodnight.

When I got home, I felt light but tired. Needless to say, I did not open the book I needed to review for my class.

The next day seemed brighter than the days before. I wasn't sure I would see Mike again on a social level, but something told me I knew darn well I would.

I remember going to work that next night at the store. It was around 8:30 p.m. when I saw him in one of our check-out lanes. I wasn't surprised. I knew he would be checking in. He was on his way out, looking all over to see if he could find me somewhere, and stopped when he saw me.

"Hey there, I didn't know if you'd be working tonight." He smiled his devilish smile at me. He knew.

"Well, here I am. Would you like to do something this weekend?" I decided to break the ice. I wanted to see him again.

"I'm on call for work, but if you want to get dinner and maybe rent a movie and watch it at my place on Friday night?"

"That sounds like a plan, I have to figure out my schedule and I'll call you later on and let you know about what time?"

"Yes, please. Have a great night!" He walked out of the store with what seemed like a pep in his step.

So, I thought about what I had going on Friday night if anything, which was really nothing. I knew my roommate Ellen would either be working or out. I should have been at the books again, but I decided to take a break and enjoy myself. I picked up the phone.

"Hi Mike. It's me. So, about Friday night, would you like to pick me up around 6:00 p.m.?" I was direct.

"Sure thing – let's go to Red Lobster."

"Sounds like a plan! See you then."

Friday came and all day, I was busy between classes and work. Mike picked me up right on time at work and off we went to Red Lobster. He did what a gentleman should do, he opened doors for me, pulled out a seat for me and had my coat hung up. I was impressed.

We ordered our dinner and drinks. We had a few laughs and some great conversation. When we finally received our dinners, I remember struggling with a shrimp that apparently went flying over the table at Mike and landed on his dinner plate. I could do nothing but laugh so loud that I managed to get the attention of the entire restaurant at that moment. I'm sure I embarrassed both of us but needless to say we had a memorable dinner.

We left and went back to his place to watch the movie that he rented which was a comedy. We had the leftover wine coolers from our meeting a couple of nights before and started to watch the movie, but we seemed to be more into each other just chatting and laughing. I felt the impulse to get to know him some more and I wanted to kiss him. So, I did. He responded very gently and then more firmly with his arms around my back. We both knew what would happen next and we both wanted it to happen. We turned off the movie and went upstairs to his bedroom where we would spend the entire weekend. It was so nice.

That Monday, I had class and came back to my own apartment in the afternoon. I think my poor roommate, Ellen, was wondering where I had been since she hadn't seen me for what seemed like an eternity. I explained to her where I was, not that I had to, but out of respect as I didn't want her to think I had abandoned our agreement. That was not my intention, and I certainly didn't know where things were going with Mike. After our discussion, I had a phone call to make and while I was on the phone there was a knock on the door. I opened the door to Mike standing there with two dozen beautiful red roses and cards from both him and Keesha (the cat). He was so thankful that I had come into his life and hoped he would see me more. I noticed Ellen's jaw drop from the kitchen. I hung up the phone to hug Mike and thank him for a wonderful time. It was a surreal moment. After he left, Ellen watched as I placed the roses into a vase. I was smiling from ear to ear, but no words were spoken. I think Ellen might have been a bit jealous. With a little pep in my step, I just went up to my room with roses and a big smile.

From then on for the next few weeks, Mike and I just had a lot of fun. We were comfortable and we enjoyed each other's company. It was about six weeks later when we began feeling serious about each other and felt very close in ways that I couldn't describe at the time. We became inseparable for the most part. I told him everything there was to know about me at the time. The good, the bad and the ugly. He genuinely cared and wanted to take care of me. Mike had met Lea briefly at the start of our relationship as she continued to pop in and out of my life. I never really understood why she wanted to see me when all my life she made it clear throughout my life that I was just a burden to her. Ever since my father, Tom, died, she seemed to keep me hidden in squalor. Mike filled that emptiness in my heart. I had met his mother, Barbara, who was a very lovely woman who gave from her heart and loved unconditionally. I realized where her son got his heart from. Barbara welcomed me and overwhelmingly loved me. I had trouble accepting that love at first because parental love was foreign to me.

About two months into our relationship when he said he wanted to be serious, we had been lying in bed one Sunday talking about our lives.

"You know, I want to tell you I'm in love with you." He said with his blue eyes glistening. You could almost hear his heart beating out of his chest.

"Really? I think I'm in love with you too". I was honest and I was shaking.

"Well, if that's how you feel…." He was being funny and abruptly rolled over.

I had looked away for just a moment to get a tissue to wipe away my tears. They were tears of joy but then I really started blubbering when I looked back at him as he was holding up a beautiful ruby and diamond ring. It wasn't a traditional engagement ring but a beautiful band-style ring.

"Will you be my wife?" he asked quietly.

"Yes...oh my God...yes, I will be your wife." I hugged him as he put the ring on my finger. It was a wonderfully happy moment.

Later the next morning, I called Lea to let her know the news. There wasn't much of a reaction, except "Well, congratulations." I think Lea was a bit envious. She never questioned whether I thought this was all too fast. I think she felt this was another way of 'getting rid' of me but not entirely because she manipulated people to get what she wanted without reciprocation.

When I told my roommate about our engagement, she seemed happy for us but later I would be told by a mutual friend how unhappy she was because I spent more time with Mike than in the apartment I was renting with her. Since I had basically moved in with Mike, Ellen ended up breaking the lease we had and moved into another apartment in the same building. She surmised I was moving on. Mike had helped me make good on my rent with her, so money was not the issue.

It turned out that she had spoken with one of my managers at the store that we both worked at. They had talked about my recent engagement and Ellen apparently made a sly comment, "you know she's only using him to foot the bill." When this came to light, I was absolutely floored not to mention *pissed*. I think she was a bit envious deep down. I called her to confront her about what she had said.

"Hey, why would you tell our manager that I'm using Mike to foot the bill?" I asked.

"Because he's paid your rent, you didn't do that" she was hasty.

"I am not using Mike at all. He's not made of money and you of all people know I am not after anyone's money. I told him I would figure things out, but he wants to do this for me and honestly Ellen, I'm in love with the man. He's a good one." There was no need to argue that point.

"Well, I'm glad you are happy. I have to go back to work now." That was the end of the conversation. We never discussed it again.

Ellen left her job at the store soon after, but somehow, we stayed friends throughout the years, and I think she came to realize how wrong she was about my relationship with Mike.

I called Sharon in Kahnawake to tell her about our engagement. She seemed to be thrilled and wanted to meet Mike. I had wanted to go to Kahnawake for Easter that year and Mike said, "let's go." He was looking forward to meeting my birth family. A few weeks later, off we went.

We took the 6-hour car ride together. It was the first time I had driven to Canada instead of taking a bus. I was elated. No more nine-hour bus trips!

We finally made it to Kahnawake, and the first thing Mike noticed on the reservation was that there were no street signs. He had never been on a reservation before.

"Um, where are the street signs? How does someone know where to go?" He was rather confused.

"Just trust me …go through the entrance tunnel and take a right at that cross." I pointed down a side road in the direction of Sharon's house. We drove by the St. Lawrence Seaway to get to the house.

Mike was just dumbfounded. I explained to him that visitors would just call from a payphone or from a store and the person they were visiting would come and get them. It was the typical thing to do on the rez. If you're lucky like me, I already knew where I was going. Still today, there are no street signs in Kahnawake. Apparently, this was normal on many reservations.

When we arrived at Sharon's house, she had other company also staying with her, including my brother, Mike. She had given us her bedroom and she would sleep in the guest room, while the other company would sleep in the living room on air mattresses or in the basement. It certainly did not matter. I just wanted the family to meet Mike.

We spent Easter weekend there. Despite my upcoming nuptials to a white man, most of the family were accepting of Mike. Well, everyone except a cousin who took me aside to explain that native people were dying out and I should consider marrying within the community to keep the Mohawk bloodline going. Through his beer breath he continued on about the benefits I would be losing by marrying a white man. Thankfully, Mike didn't hear this conversation and honestly, I took it with a grain of salt. Nothing could change my intentions.

Michelle Rice Gauvreau

CHAPTER 10 – LOVE & MARRIAGE

October 1991-My Marriage

Mike and I were married within eight months of meeting. Sometimes I wonder if I rushed into the marriage aka adulthood as an escape from my childhood and Lea's crosshairs. We had our ups and downs throughout our courtship, and it was like we had solidified our lives together without really enjoying much in between. It was tough to plan our wedding. I had wanted a May wedding the following year but Mike wanted it sooner than that. He wanted a small wedding, and I wanted something more grandiose. I wanted to show the world that someone really does love me. We had arguments about the wedding, the cost, and who we were going to invite. As the financial reality hit, I settled for a small wedding in October 1991.

Surprisingly, Lea actually stepped up and agreed to pay for the wedding dinner, probably her way of keeping some control over me. Possibly part of her manipulative ways. While planning the wedding, Lea insisted that I not invite my birth family there, nor my foster parents, Geoff and Elaine. I felt that was unfair but also surprisingly, I did as I was commanded. One of Lea's brothers, Uncle Paul, was invited as was her sister, Shirley. Uncle Moe and his wife Rita, however, were not invited. There were still hard feelings between Lea and Rita for telling me the truth as a teenager, and I suppose I was brainwashed into believing Rita was bad. As the dysfunction continued amongst family members, my Aunt Shirley, who was driving up from Florida, demanded that I not invite her own daughters. I felt trapped. In the end, I only had 11 people attend my wedding. I was a little disappointed not having my dream wedding.

As I woke up on our wedding morning, I was alone with my thoughts. I had sent Mike to his mother's as I was trying to hold on to some sort of tradition that the groom wasn't supposed to see the bride until the actual wedding. I had a bagel breakfast ready for Lea, me and my maid of honor, Bonnie, who was a friend from the store. Despite being anxious, we had a nice morning of exchanging pleasantries. When it was time to get my hair done, Lea drove me to the salon. In typical Lea fashion, She attempted to embarrass me by telling everyone I was 'snapping at her.' The stylists ignored her. I was relieved. Some things never change.

While I was getting my hair done, Lea walked over to a nearby store and bought herself a pair of earrings for the wedding. I never saw her wear jewelry before. She was not one to be fancy, but I guess she wanted to look good on the big day.

After I got my hair done, Lea dropped me off at my place so I could get dressed for the wedding. She went home to get ready herself. She only lived a few minutes away from me.

"I'll be back for you in an hour," she said.
"That's cutting it close Mom, please try to hurry up"
"Don't rush me…I'm paying for your wedding dinner."

I shut my mouth and went inside. Ugh! I should have just nodded my head.

While I was changing, I started having doubts about my outfit. I had bought a nice white sequined jumpsuit and a nice pair of sparkling white shoes. Over the months that I planned my wedding, I wanted a beautiful wedding gown but given the events that ensued during the planning I figured a simple outfit would suffice. I always regretted not wearing a traditional gown on my wedding day.

After I was dressed, the clock kept ticking away. I knew Lea would take her time, so I called her.

"Are you coming to get me?" I asked abruptly without saying hello first.
"Yes – I'm almost ready." I knew she wasn't fussing with getting ready, she was just procrastinating.

I hung up the phone at that point hoping she would be back in a short amount of time. I paced around my living room until then. I was anxious. Am I doing the right thing? I'm just 22 years old.

Finally, the buzzer from the lobby made some noise. She was there. I came out. Lea did look nice in her suit. I had on my outfit but getting into her car suddenly made me nauseous. The smell from the cigarettes felt like it was asphyxiating me. I should have been used to it by now, but I wasn't. My anxiety was on overload at this point.

"Mom, we need to hustle to Uncle Paul's." I knew we were supposed to go over to his house before the ceremony. I guess he wanted to drive us as 'his family' to the Church.

We made it in the nick of time with a few minutes to spare while my Uncle Bill (Aunt Shirley's husband) was setting up his camcorder to record the ceremony for me. Uncle Bill was always so kind to me. I think he knew I did not have a good life with Lea so he stepped in from time-to-time when he could, just to be there.

Everyone complimented me on how beautiful I looked. I took it all in stride while still gasping on second-hand cigarettes and cigar smoke from Lea and her siblings. Oh, how my family just didn't seem to care about any of that, but I guess it was the era. It just wasn't something you thought about back in those days.

When it came time to go, we all piled into Uncle Paul's car and he drove us to the Church.

We made it to the Church just in time. I saw my friend Bonnie and her fiancé Brian just pulling in and I immediately felt less stressed. When I stepped out of the car, I went around and kissed everyone in the Church parking lot thanking them for being there. It was time to go in as I knew Mike and his mother, Barbara, would be arriving soon. I wanted to stay out of sight until the wedding started.

Everyone followed me into the side door of the Church, and I hid in a closet as Mike walked in. He eventually told me that he could see me, and I told him he shouldn't have been looking. Barbara, my mother-in-law, pulled him into the Church to get things started. The minister and his wife came by and reiterated our plans to me as to when I would come out to meet Mike at the altar.

The sanctuary was quiet. There was no music as I walked down the Church aisle by myself. Lea didn't walk with me, and my uncles didn't walk with me. I was alone.

As I got to the altar, I saw Mike looking at me with tears in his eyes. He took my hands very tightly, promising me he'd never let go. My friend Bonnie stood right beside me for support at the altar holding our wedding rings as the minister read our vows which we recited again to each other with the obligatory "I dos." Literally, within eight minutes, we were married. That was it. No big deal, no music, and no clapping. It was almost too quiet. When we turned around, everyone came up to congratulate and hug us, I felt a sort of euphoria that the weight of the world had been lifted off somehow. This is where I would begin leaving my childhood behind to become an adult creating a new life.

We realized we did not even bring a camera to our wedding. Thankfully, Bonnie's fiancé, Brian, had a camera in his car and he saved the day for us by taking some nice pictures.

Due to the Church's rules, my Uncle Bill wasn't allowed to take video while the ceremony was taking place, but he would take video afterward. I was grateful to both of them for helping us out.

Afterward, we went to our wedding dinner at an expensive restaurant several towns away. We got into our respective cars and Mike led the way. Lea joined us in our car. The minister and his wife came to the dinner as well. Our table was in a small private room and was decorated very nicely. The waitress explained our menus and had stories about the restaurant to tell. I don't remember the exact story, but we were told the restaurant was haunted. Fitting for the weekend before Halloween. Everyone seemed fascinated by this and the fact that we chose such a cool place for our wedding dinner.

We had a delicious meal and some wedding cake together. We were all lost in conversation when it became very late. We knew it was time for us to get home, but we needed to drop my mother-in-law off first. Barbara was so happy for her son. I assured her I would do my best for him. As I watched her smile lovingly at Mike, I wished my father, Tom, could have been there to witness the day. Lea, on the other hand, never extended love to her daughter. As a matter of fact, she even gloated a bit when she showed me the dinner bill. It was one of the few things she ever did for me so why she felt the need to rub it in my face, I'll never know. Perhaps she was saving face in front of her siblings.

When we got home where we ascended to bed almost immediately falling asleep, waking into our married life. The next morning, we were both pretty tired from all the excitement the night before. We took our time leaving to go to Niagara Falls for our honeymoon, thankful we didn't have to rush.

It was a nice quiet drive to Canadian side of the falls. We enjoyed some of the sites and took pictures especially of the falls and of course fell into some of the tourist traps like 'Ripley's Believe It or Not' and an arcade where we became kids again playing pinball games. We did some shopping at the local outlet stores. We stayed at a local motel. We walked around the nearby park. We ate well at some local diners known for their cuisine and we up to the famous Skylon Tower to look over the falls from the observation deck. Suddenly it occurred to me that 22 years ago, I was just a little Indian baby born on a reservation not far from where I was standing. As I gazed at the horizon over Canada, I thought about my birth mother, Sharon, and wondered if I would ever meet my birth father.

One of the best and funniest parts of the trips was when I was standing right by the rushing Horseshoe Falls and I said to Mike, "you know, all that water gushing down over the falls makes me want to go in and experience that feeling." I was joking, not realizing there was an elderly gentleman standing next to us listening.

"Hey! Be a gentleman and help her up!" this stranger said to my husband so seriously, but you could see the glimmer in his eye and knew that he was teasing.

All I could do was laugh and Mike made the comment, "if it weren't illegal, I might just help her."

"Oh, he knows better!" I just laughed it off.

From there, we left Niagara Falls and all its grandeur and drove down through Vermont to take in the scenery and shops. It really was a nice albeit short honeymoon with good memories.

We returned home and settled into married life. We went back to work, he as superintendent of our apartment building and me as a cashier at the retail store. I continued attending community college where I would eventually graduate with an associate degree. I had future aspirations of doing something involving law.

Although our routines helped normalize our new life together, married life wasn't all that easy. We had a lot of arguments. We argued about finances, household chores, the time spent at my school, work, and my social life. I liked going out with my friends on occasion. Mike was older than me and much more traditional. He was trying to teach me his way of doing things or his way of thinking what I should be doing as his wife versus what I was doing. I was simply trying to find my own way, unsure of my new role as a wife. Our age gap was evident.

While we spent time together at home, I longed to go out as a couple. I just wanted to have some fun. Although Mike could be a wise cracking joker at any event, he wasn't much of a social butterfly. We didn't go out much, against the grain of my independent native spirit. I often wondered if I was capable of ever being tamed.

1992 A Sibling Surprise

One morning, Mike dropped me off at Lea's house, because her station wagon had broken down and she needed help moving boxes from the car to the garage. As I greeted her with a hot cup of coffee from McDonald's (I knew she did not have a coffee maker) I rolled my eyes as I glanced at the stacks of old McDonald's coffee cups laying around the house along with the hoard. Wow! She still doesn't throw anything away. I may never fully understand hoarding other than it can be symptom of mental illness.

I went back out to the driveway to start moving yet even more boxes of junk when a pile of unopened mail fell to the floor. One of the envelopes struck me as peculiar. It was a large letter-sized envelope with Lea's name and address handwritten. The return address was from Maryland, also handwritten.

"Mom, what's this envelope?" I curiously asked.
"Oh I don't know..." Lea avoided the question.
"It's from Maryland, do you know anyone down there?" I was not giving up yet.
"Yes, but it's none of your business..." A familiar answer resounded from Lea's.
"Are you sure? Daddy worked in Baltimore." I quipped back. "May I open this?" I pleaded. Something told me this was

something that I needed to know. I just had a feeling, but I didn't know what it was.

"Oh fine. I don't care." She finally realized I wasn't giving up.

"Okay." I proceeded to open the envelope, as I did, Lea watched me carefully. Why was I feeling that same knot in my stomach as I did when I first found out I was adopted.

It turned out to be someone trying to connect with our family. It was an emotional letter written by a woman named Denise from Baltimore. As I read through her words out loud, my mouth dropped, and my eyes widened. She was Tom's biological daughter. Apparently, many years ago, while on a business trip, while he was married to his first wife, Tomasina, Tom started an affair with Denise's mother. Denise was born from that relationship.

Denise's letter took my breath away. I immediately wanted to call her. My fingers shook as I dialed the rotary phone. I left a message on the answering machine. She was my father's only biological child and she too had so few memories of him. It didn't seem fair. I looked at Lea who seemed very upset that this had come to light. As it turned out, she knew about Denise and never bothered to tell me about her. Another secret. In the back of my mind, I thought Denise must have felt like she lost everything the year Tom passed away. I felt her pain.

Who Am I? I'm the sister of two siblings.

1992-1993 Baby News

Just before we celebrated our one-year anniversary of wedding bliss, we found out I was pregnant. Funny story really.

We had gone to The Big E (New England's Largest Fair). Lea joined us at the time. Since my wedding day, she seemed to accept me on a more adult level but I felt I was always on 'alert' status with her. I never fully trusted what she might do or say, but in my heart, I knew she didn't have anyone else. In a weird way, after all I went through with her, I felt sorry for her.

While at the Big E, Lea and I went into the circus tent to the circus. After we found seats, I felt claustrophobic. and I wanted to faint. I had never felt like that in my life. I panicked. I felt like I could see auras around people. That was scary. I ran out of the tent and into the fresh air. I had to find Mike quickly and luckily found him nearby. I ran into his arms crying. He was not sure what was going on with me. He must have assumed it was another argument with my mother. I was a hot mess!

"What's the matter?!" he asked, looking at me, very concerned.

"I almost fainted in there!" I cried.

"Oh no you didn't." He loved to downplay my reaction to things sometimes.

"Yes, she did Mike," Lea said walking out behind me, looking very serious.

He took a look at me and agreed. I looked pale and we left. I hated cutting the day short as I loved this fair so much.

"Honey, do you think you're pregnant?" He asked as we got in the car.

"I'm not sure babe." I replied almost in a whisper.

When we started to drive out of the parking lot, Mike turned to me and asked, "should we swing by the pharmacy?"

"Yes, we probably should." I answered trying to hold back my nausea.

I froze, unsure of what to think. We hadn't given much thought about having children so soon, but I knew we needed to get a pregnancy test.

It was a quiet ride back home. Mike had the radio on just to break the silence in the car. I started to get a bit emotional, not really wanting to talk as each time I tried to say something, I could feel my throat start to close and my eyes welled up a few times. I stared out the window watching the highway scenery go by. As if I wasn't tense enough, Lea began sighing loudly, as if we were disrupting her day. She probably just needed a cigarette. She said she wanted to get home. She didn't seem to care about my situation. I never understood why she was so coldhearted. Maybe because she could never have her own children. I'm not sure I ever counted as her own daughter. At only 22 years old, I've already gone through so much trauma with her.

We stopped at the pharmacy to pick up the pregnancy test. Mike and Lea waited in the car as I ran in. I didn't want anyone overwhelming me as I made the purchase. At the time, the tests were very expensive, and we were already financially strapped.

When we returned to our apartment parking lot, Lea got out of the car running to her own car desperate for a cigarette. She left to go home almost immediately. I wasn't surprised she didn't want to stay for a while although it would have been nice for her to stick around long enough to find out the results of the test. I think she was probably feeling conflicted about me possibly being pregnant. We waved her off and went into the apartment.

As soon as we opened the door, I lied down on the couch for a while. I needed to rest. It was hard to close my eyes and relax as my mind was swirling. My heart started beating fast in anticipation of me taking that test. I eventually mustered the courage and went into the bathroom. It would be the longest three minutes of my life. After time was up, I looked at the test results.

"Honey – it's positive." I burst into tears and felt faint at the same time. Was this real? Oh God! I was not sure I was ready.

"Ok, well now we have to go to the doctor and get the actual blood test done." He was stone-faced. He never really reacted to the initial news of the home pregnancy test. He believed that home tests weren't always 100% accurate. I was blubbering actually trying to absorb the news because I already knew in my heart, I was pregnant, and I somehow felt that our baby would be a boy.

The next morning, I called the doctor's office and they put in the order for a blood test that day and off we went into the city talking about how our life was about to change.

"If the blood test comes back positive, you're going to have to stay home after the baby is born." Mike insisted on being the traditional guy he was.

"I know, you've said this before." I knew we would need to plan carefully, and it would be hard financially, emotionally and physically.

Was it just me? Did all young couples go through the same hardships when starting a family of their own? Never having a 'real family,' I would carry this angst with me for months.

"Let's wait to make plans when the blood test comes back." I was nervous. I was in a state of all the what-ifs. What if I am really pregnant? What if things don't go right? What if I lose the baby? I was not ready for what was next. My head couldn't stop spinning that day and I could barely sleep that night.

The test results came back the next day. I was at work when the message came through on the answering machine at home. Mike called me as I was ringing customers out at the store.

"Hey Hon, there's a message on the machine, do you want me to play it now?" He was finally nervous as reality was about to hit, positive or negative. He could see on the caller ID that it was the doctor's office number.

"Um...nah, let's wait until I get home." In the back of my mind, I knew he wasn't going to wait. He would play it and set it back to where he could act like he didn't play the message and pick me up knowing the answer.

"Wait! OK, just play it." Since I was waiting for a price check at my register, I figured I may as well hear it now.

"Hi Michelle, this is Cindy at the doctor's office. Great news! Your pregnancy test came back positive. You will need to make an appointment with our office to follow-up on all your prenatal care and visit with each of the doctors. Call us back when you can. Talk to you soon. Oh, and CONGRATULATIONS!" Cindy seemed jovial. My knees buckled and I felt dizzy for a moment. Mike and I were in shock. Well wow! Ohhh, there goes my head spinning again.

"I'll pick you up at closing time." Mike said.

"Ok, I'll see you then." I wasn't sure what to say at that moment.

The customer waiting on the price check stood at my register looking at me "Are you ok, you look like you've seen a ghost."

"I just found out I'm pregnant" I was nervously fidgeting with the register trying to input the SKU numbers to get the price of the customer's item.

"Well, congratulations!" She paid and left. This particular customer would end up coming back to the store from time to time to check on me throughout my pregnancy. I loved my regular customers.

When Mike picked me up at work that night, I could see his face as I walked to the car. He laughed nervously like he didn't know what had just hit him. We were both stunned by the news. I was overwhelmed. I was going to be a mother. Me, the girl who never really had a loving mother herself, was now going to have a child. In that next moment, I swore that I would never raise this baby the way I was raised.

Moving forward, I had a fairly easy pregnancy. Whenever Mike had to work and because I didn't have a driver's license at the time, Lea actually offered to bring me to my prenatal appointments. My relationship with her was a rollercoaster of emotions. Some days she seemed to want to be a part of my life but other days not so much. I took whatever I could get. After all these years, I somehow still longed for acceptance from my mother, especially now that I was about to become a mother myself.

One day, before one of my ultrasound appointments, Lea showed up at our apartment. It just so happened to be the same day we were going to find out if we were having a boy or a girl. Mike just shrugged his shoulders and let her come with us. When we arrived at the doctors' office, the three of us crowded into the little examination room. It's a boy! To my surprise, Lea had some tears. I'm not sure if they were tears of joy or tears of sadness because she couldn't have a baby of her own due to multiple miscarriages/unknown health issues. I never asked her.

As the months went on, my morning sickness turned into night sickness, and I was ballooning like a big butterball turkey feeling self-conscious about the way I looked. I felt like I waddled like a duck. I thought for sure I would have a big baby.

I was given two baby showers. The first one by my foster parents, Geoff and Elaine, who stood by me through thick and thin as a teenager. They chose not to invite Lea and I knew it was because of the way Lea had treated me in the past. It was really a special day. I was surrounded by many Native American friends that I bonded with through our years in the Powwow Society. I smiled as I scanned the room and promised myself, I would raise my son to know his native roots which were rich in culture and family. I felt like I belonged. I knew then that my son would never face a loveless childhood like I did.

A week before I gave birth, the second baby shower was given by my mother-in-law, Barbara, which Lea kindly paid for half, despite having no family from her side attend. The restaurant luncheon consisted mostly of Barbara's cousins and friends from Church. My birth mother Sharon in Canada was not invited to either baby shower. I know that she lived far away but a part of me wished she could have been there to experience the joy.   I was given so many lovely gifts for the baby, something I was never used to having as a child.

The day before I gave birth, I was not feeling well at all. Mike and I had been out all day with my mother-in-law running errands. The baby wasn't due for another month. My feet were incredibly swollen and looked like elephant feet. I just felt off. I wanted to go home, lay on the sofa and watch a movie. I was exhausted.

That same night/early morning, at about 2:00 a.m., I thought I was dreaming that I had wet the bed, but it wasn't a dream. My water broke. I started to panic. I didn't wake Mike yet as I didn't want him going into panic mode then. We hadn't even put the crib together. Nothing was ready. Could this really be happening now? My stomach felt tight. I was nervous. I went into the bathroom and realized my water really did break. I called the doctor's office and was told that I needed to go to the hospital right away to be examined.

"Mike! Wake up honey!" I whispered.
"What's up babe?" He said barely awake.
"Don't roll over, the bed is wet!" I exclaimed.
"What? Are you ok?" He jumped up.
"I'm ok – we have to go to the hospital now. I think my water broke," I explained hurriedly.
"Ok, ok, let's get dressed and I'll go get the car!" He rushed to get dressed and ran out.

I put my clothes on fast and only grabbed my keys. I went down to the building lobby where Mike was waiting for me. My stomach was still feeling weirdly tight.

We arrived at the hospital in record time as my husband had the pedal to the metal and he was tempted to drive over a set of railroad tracks as his father did to his mother when she was in labor with him. I thought that would be keeping with family tradition, but thankfully he decided against the idea. My belly was feeling tighter and tighter.

We arrived at the labor and delivery unit where I sat in the waiting area with several other expectant moms. Finally, after several hours, they did an ultrasound which indicated I did lose my water but that I would need to be induced because my son's head was not in the down position. They needed to make sure he turned into position first. I was asked if I wanted an epidural for the pain, but I said no at the time and that I wanted a natural birth. Oh, how wrong I was!

A few hours later after being induced, the contractions came on strong but far apart. The baby had not moved much. They increased the Pitocin they gave me causing multiple contractions.

"Honey, are you doing, ok?" Mike would ask gently.

"No, I think I need the epidural!" I was out of breath trying to breathe correctly.

"It might be too late at this point" he said, a little scared of me.

"GIVE ME THE FUCKING DRUGS NOW!" It was as if I were possessed by the devil. The nurse ran out to find the doctor who called in the orders for an epidural, stat. Thank God it wasn't too late!

The anesthesiologist came running in with what I was begging for. She had to put a pain block in my spine. I sat up and the nurse was annoyed with my very long hair and had to find a hair band. I didn't care at the moment. The procedure did not work the first time, so a second epidural was done. Finally, some relief. But, the second epidural proved to be a bit too much. I was more than comfortably numb; I was frozen from my waist down. I couldn't feel the lower half of my body, nor could I feel my contractions although they were showing up on the monitor.

"Um, why aren't you doing your Lamaze breathing?" my nurse would ask me.

"Because I can't feel anything right now, not even my legs." I was sarcastic. I was not in the mood for anyone at that point and ready to take on anyone coming at me as the Mohawk warrior woman I was living up to.

Mike left to go get lunch. He was exhausted that my labor was not progressing as fast as he would have liked.

People were coming in and out trying to give me suggestions to move things along which included getting up and walking. I swiftly reminded them that I couldn't feel my legs from the two epidurals and would probably fall down after one step. So, all the suggestions went nowhere.

A slow few hours later, Mike left again to get some dinner. The nursing staff changed shifts and I now had my Lamaze teacher as my primary nurse for the evening. While I know she meant well, she kept lecturing me about using my 'candle breaths' and all that she taught us. She wanted Mike to jump on the bed with me and hold me from behind to help the baby move further into position. I was not comfortable with that and declined. She thought I would need oxygen, so she gave me a mask which I immediately ripped off. I was just 23 years old and apparently, a lost cause in active labor.

To make things worse, I heard another woman screaming down the hall which added to my fear. This was something I wanted no part of.

"Unhook me please and get me a wheelchair, I'm going home!" I was serious.

"You can't get out of here now, you're about to have a baby!" The nurse laughed. There was no way out of this now.

"Seriously, I'm not doing this!" I was really desperate.

"You know, Dr. Olsen, just delivered four babies all at once. He was running and sliding into each room," one of the other nurses said, looking at me like I was next, and I was.

My contractions were getting larger, and they still could be seen on the monitor. Why I wasn't doing my breathing was beyond my nurse's comprehension. She had been our Lamaze teacher throughout my last trimester.

"Michelle, please do your breathing correctly like I taught you, it will help you in the long run." She was not happy with me. This would not be my moment to make her proud. I was a Lamaze failure! Mike suddenly piped in.

"You know, she can't feel the contractions right now and honestly, your breathing techniques went out the window hours ago." Mike said firmly. Unfortunately, that made her ignore us for the rest of the night. Unless she was spoken to or had to check on me, she had nothing to say as far as any conversation with us. The tension was thick from there until I gave birth.

It was around 7:00 p.m. when I could finally feel a contraction but still could not move my legs as they felt numb. The nurse and doctor had to put my legs in stirrups, but Mike wanted to hold my right leg out which had provided some comfort.

As the nurse checked me, I started dilating very fast and the baby finally moved into position. She wanted me to start pushing. I was worried my baby would turn into a breech baby like I was, but he decided not to do that. Phew!

"Mike, if you want to look, the baby is crowning," the nurse said.

Mike looked at me in tears, "I see the head, honey." He became filled with emotion.

"Great...get him out of me!" I screamed. I was more than annoyed after being in labor for so many hours. The nurses, the doctors, my husband...all of them could go straight to hell at that moment. I was so exhausted.

Finally, I gave one or two more big pushes, and my son was born in front of about 16 people. It was a teaching hospital with several resident obstetric and pediatric students observing. Being a premature baby, many staff members were also present.

The doctor put my son on stomach, and I picked him up not thinking about anything but seeing him. My son was beautiful. He looked so much like Mike at that moment when he was a newborn. He was a healthy 6 lb. 2 oz baby born on May 2, 1993, at 9:14 p.m. The baby team was on hand to check him out and made sure everything was good. It was. That was a very rough 18 hours, but I can certainly empathize with so many mothers who have gone through labor longer than that.

Mike called his mother who I am sure was a nervous wreck waiting to hear from us. He had called her periodically throughout the day to update her on my progress. We had only called Lea once, on our way to the hospital, but didn't follow-up with her until the next day.

We named our son, Raymond, after Mike's father. My mother-in-law was happily surprised that we did that. Afterall, Mike wanted to honor his father whom he missed so much.

After I was moved to my maternity room, Mike ended up driving home that night in tears. He didn't want to leave us but there was a lot of work to be done at home. He knew he had to put the crib together as we did not plan on the baby coming so early. He had his 'honey-do' list and managed to get everything done before I came home with the baby.

Two days later, walking into our home with baby Raymond, our cat didn't know what to think of him. She just kept staring at him in his bassinet and would run whenever he made a noise. It was quite funny, and a needed distraction. The apartment felt different now. I couldn't believe I was now a mother. I was scared. What now? I knew I would have to lean on my husband a lot.

Ray would be the only child we would have. Motherhood introduced me to new layers of emotions I never knew existed.

As we had previously decided, I quit my job after my maternity leave at the store to stay home and raise my son. I planned on going back to work when Ray got to kindergarten. The whole concept of staying home for five years was a tough decision for us because we desperately needed the money. Mike, however, believed that mothers should stay home to raise their children.

The Meeting of the Two Mothers

As Ray was about 10 months old, I had been talking to my birth mother, Sharon, about coming down to meet her grandson. She was on the fence about traveling to Connecticut because of work obligations. She started working as a butcher in a local market in Kahnawake. When my brother, Mike, offered to drive her down, she decided to take the time off to meet her new grandson. She already had one grandson, Frankie, Mike's son. My brother married about two years after I did.

I was thrilled they were finally coming to see us. I then had to tell Lea about Sharon coming to visit. I wanted them to meet each other but, wasn't sure how well it would turn out. Lea could turn nasty on a dime. As unpredictable as Lea always was, she took the news surprisingly well.

It was a cloudy day when Sharon and my brother arrived late one afternoon a couple weeks later. I was nervous. It was the first time I would be hosting my birth family. I wanted things to be perfect. As my brother settled in on the sofa from the long drive, Sharon sat at our dining room table drinking a beer. I decided to go upstairs to see if Ray was waking up from his afternoon nap. My brother followed me and looked at Ray in his crib sound asleep. He told me to let him sleep. I did, for a few more minutes.

As Ray started to wake up, I picked him up, hugging him and kissing him. I tiptoed with him in my arms back down the stairs to have him meet his native grandmother and his uncle. It was a beautiful moment. Sharon cried as I put him in her lap. She looked so happy. I took pictures of the two of them together. Ray rested his little head on Sharon's chest as if to say, 'I love her.' It was such a moving moment. Even the pictures I took could never fully describe that moment. I knew they would have a good bond together and that was priceless to me at the time.

The next morning after everyone got a good night's sleep, we had to go to the bank as Sharon needed to exchange some Canadian money for American money. The return on the money at the time was not what she expected. It was lower than the going rate, but it seemed as if we didn't have a choice. It was ok, anything Sharon needed if she didn't have enough money, we would cover for her. Afterall, she covered for me when I visited Canada.

After we got back to my place, my brother took me aside to explain he needed to go back to Canada for a few days and would pick up our mother sometime the following week. He seemed stressed about finances for supporting his own family. It felt like he couldn't catch a break at the time. I felt bad for him. He was sniffling a lot and I assumed he was coming down with a cold. It was better he wasn't around my baby if he was getting sick. My brother left the next morning to go back home. Sharon stayed with us another week.

I made plans with Lea to come over to pick us up for lunch the next day. As she pulled into the in the driveway, you could see the back of her station wagon was filled to the brim with stuff. It was obvious that her hoarding tendencies had crossed over into her vehicle. It was as if she ran out of room in her house, and the car was just another storage place for her. I was embarrassed but hoped that Sharon would understand. I had told her about Lea's hoarding.

I had Sharon sit in the front seat while I piled into the back putting Ray in the car seat after I pushed away some clutter.

I held back my frustration over bringing the baby into this dirty nasty smoke-filled car. I don't think the smoke bothered Sharon because she smoked like a chimney herself.

"Mom, please meet Sharon," I said while buckling Ray into the car seat, "Sharon, please meet Lea."
"Hello Lea." Sharon was incredibly shy.
"Hello Sharon, it's so nice to finally meet you." Lea said enthusiastically.

Huh? Wait, was this Lea? As I watched her face beaming, I felt like I was in the twilight zone for a moment. Lea was being polite. I didn't trust her.

They hit it off well. Wow! They talked about Kahnawake and Sharon asked if Lea would like some cigarettes from Kahnawake. Well of course she did, and Sharon gave her a baggie of cigarettes from her purse as a gift for Lea. I had no idea that Sharon was going to do that, but I think it was an old Mohawk custom that people honor their elders in the form of tobacco. Sharon did so in thanks to Lea for raising me.

As the day went on, Lea drove us all over town. They talked about Sharon's job at the time as a meat cutter in the local market back home. Lea said to Sharon that if she ever moved to the States, the money for a meat cutter would be much higher than she was making at the time. Sharon was impressed and I think she may have considered it for a moment.

We ended up dropping Sharon off at a local hairdresser to her hair cut at her request. It gave me and Lea some time to grab coffee and chat. I was dying to know what she was thinking.

"So, it seems like you like her." I said.
"What makes you think I wouldn't like Sharon?" She replied a bit sarcastic, as was her nature.

"Gee Mom, why don't you tell me?" I snapped at her thinking about our less than positive past conversations about Kahnawake and Tom's family.

She glared back at me but never responded. We just drank our coffees and figured things would be better if we both just shut up.

After Sharon was done getting her hair cut, we went to the local mall and had lunch together in the food course. We walked around the stores where Sharon bought a few items for herself and a toy or two for Ray. We all sat and watched Ray in the kids' play area. He was just learning how to walk so it was a perfect setting for the grandmothers to see him being active. I remember that moment being so surreal. My two mothers together in the same space where I was now a mother with my son. Would this ever happen again? I had no idea. I wanted to cherish those fleeting seconds. It was as if for one moment I didn't feel rejected. After a lifetime of feeling guarded and unprotected I suddenly felt calm and secure with my family dynamics at the moment.

The day was a success after all. My two mothers were together for the first time and possibly the last. Lea, who had never been nice to anyone who showed interest in me was surprisingly cordial. Lea was friendly toward Sharon and that was all that mattered.

A few days later, my brother drove back down to Connecticut to pick up Sharon. She seemed so attached to her new grandson, Ray, that I suspected that she didn't want to leave, but I knew she had to get back to her family in Kahnawake. I promised her we would come visit soon and she would come back. I would learn later through Sharon that my brother actually brought a vile of cocaine with him which pissed me off, but I never said anything. I was incensed that he would bring drugs into my home.

Going Back to School

When Ray was about a year old, I really wanted to go back to school to obtain my paralegal certification, but Mike was worried about how it would impact our finances. It took me a while to convince him that this would be the right step for both of us. He agreed so long as I was sure I would get the loans or grants needed for the business school I had in mind. I applied and got into the paralegal program. My commitment had to be a year of night school so Mike could watch Ray. While at school, I was finally able to make some new friends. It was a great class. We were very supportive of each other. I learned so much that I was certain I would make a good paralegal once my son was in school full time. I graduated with honors and was proud of myself knowing that I had an associate degree and now a paralegal certificate. I was unstoppable. For the first time in my life, I felt confident. Neither my birth parents nor my adoptive parents were college educated. I felt worthy. I was actually proud of myself as a wife, a mother and a strong woman. Strong like bull!

Who Am I? I am an educated woman!

After graduation, Mike had the idea of wanting to move back to his hometown, a few towns over, where the schools were better, and we could be closer to his mother. When Ray was about a year old, we made the move. Our new condominium came with Mike's new job. It was a lovely building complex behind a beautiful town park filled with floral gardens and flowering trees. Mike now worked as a superintendent of our building. It was a smart move. I came to love my new town and met so many people along the way.

I was still a stay-at-home wife and mom, not yet working, I decided to start a transcription business from home where I would transcribe documents for local doctors and lawyers. I found a few clients that were steady, and the money helped pay for some bills and food.

After my son started kindergarten full-time, one of my clients ended up hiring me to work at his law office. I worked for this attorney for the next five years and I was grateful for that. I learned about the legal world which gave me a steppingstone for my next job. My future was looking for a whole lot brighter. I still work as a legal professional today now in one of the most prestigious law firms in the country.

CHAPTER 11 –MEETING MY BIRTH FATHER

1999

Ever since meeting my birth mother's family and getting to know them, there was one thing that always bothered me: finding my birth father. Sharon and my grandmother sensed that I felt that void. I longed to see his face. To hear his voice. Fifteen years after first meeting my birth mother, I would finally meet *the* man.

Meeting Eddie was something of a dream at first. I was 15 when I first learned his full name. When I was in Canada that summer, I tried to find him to no avail pre internet days. I had been waiting to put a face to the man that made me. I was determined and utilized what tools I had available to try and find him on my own. Little did I know he was living in a neighboring town right next to Kahnawake all these years. So close, yet so far. My grandmother, Mary, did not want me to ever find or meet him. She said I would only get hurt. As a teenager, I didn't want to hear that and even as an adult I still wanted to know who he was. I tried so many times to find him but failed. I wondered if he ever thought of me. I also wondered if he was still alive. Sure enough, I would get the surprise of my life later one night, fifteen years later, at the age of 30.

Not much was really known about this man. Sharon was dating him for a short time between 1968 – 1969 before he married a woman named Sandra. Eddie and Sandra both had friends in Kahnawake, and both were well known there. Rumor had it that Sandra and her father at the time were connected to some influential "bosses" and that Eddie was forced to marry Sandra by contract. I don't know if there was any truth to that.

Before that, I was conceived, and Eddie knew about it. He took off to marry Sandra anyway. When he learned that I had been born, he showed up at my grandmother's house to see Sharon. She showed him a picture of me. She explained that she had to give me up. Apparently, he immediately went into the bathroom, closed the door, and didn't come out for a while. When he emerged, he looked very pale and sullen, like he had been crying. Sharon said they exchanged good-byes and he left quietly. That was the last time Sharon saw him until 30 years later.

When I was happily married, with a family of my own, I finally met him. I wanted nothing from him. I would hear stories whenever I visited Kahnawake that he was around and that he had owned a trucking business while working at a train depot in Montreal. My brother, Mike, had met him once at a nearby industrial park and drove me there one day to look for him. We couldn't find Eddie. I was disappointed but knew one day it would happen.

I was up late one night on the computer scrolling the internet when I was startled by the phone ringing. I saw that it was Sharon calling so I immediately picked up the phone.

"Hello?" I answered surprised.
"Michelle!!!" I could tell Sharon was feeling good, which meant she had had a few beers that night.
"What's wrong?" I assumed something was wrong.
"I found your father!" Her voice exuded excitement.
My heart jumped.
"What?!" I wasn't sure if she was joking but she was never one to kid around about this situation. She knew what it would mean to me.
"Okay...who, how, what, when?" I was stunned and nearly dropped the phone. I wanted all the details. God, please tell me!

"Your cousin Ryan is dating his daughter, Tina" she proceeded to give me the details.

It had come to light that his daughter was dating one of my native cousins. Because Sharon knew this was a direct connection to my birth father, she called me. She always vowed to help if she could. She certainly did.

"Tina's father *is* your father," she continued.

"Are you sure? Can you get a phone number for me?" I was excited but didn't want to wake my family.

"I'm working on that for you. I promised you I would help you find him, and I'll get you the information."

"I know you did. Thank you." I was shaking and almost in tears.

She went on to say that she had asked Ryan about this, and he confirmed that he was indeed dating Tina and her father was Eddie and her mother was a woman named Sandra. Sharon was shocked. She told Ryan that Eddie was my father. He was in shock as well. She asked Ryan to get a telephone number and he came through with the number but asked that I talk to Tina first. Ryan had told Tina about me. Sharon said she was stunned to say the least and wanted to believe Ryan but had a hard time accepting the story. I, of course, agreed that I would talk to her first.

It took me a few days to call Tina as I was still in shock and very nervous. I was actually more scared to call Tina than I was calling Sharon when I was 15. I figured she would be in denial that her father could possibly have another daughter.

"Hello?" an older lady answered. I knew it wasn't Tina. I assumed it was Sandra.

"Hello, may I please speak to Tina?"

"Who's calling?" Another question…

"Michelle," I said plainly.

"Sure, here she is," Sandra was polite.

"Hello?" Tina answered.

"Hi Tina, my name is Michelle. I'm Ryan's cousin. I know he's told you the story about me," I explained.

"Hold on, ok? I have to move into the other room." She didn't want her mother to hear her. Sandra didn't know yet.

"Yes, he did, but I don't think we're related." She expressed a sharp tone.

"I beg to differ Tina; my mother Sharon wouldn't lie about anything. As a matter of fact, when she learned your last name matched your father's and the timeline of their past relationship, she immediately put two and two together. Your father *is* my father. That's pretty compelling if I do say so myself." I explained.

Tina seemed to have calmed down and I was relieved. I explained a few more things, especially about how I knew who her father was married to and soon she seemed to finally accept the fact that I might be related after all.

"Tina, I'll send you a letter and some pictures if that is ok?" I offered.

"Fine, here's the address." That was the extent of our conversation at that point.

I sent out a letter with some pictures to her in care of Sharon's mailing address so Ryan could give it to her. Tina didn't want to alarm her parents. I respected that.

We spoke soon after she received the letter.

"I got your letter and photos, I'm still not convinced of things – you spelled our last name wrong," she said.

"Hey, I'm not making this up." You know my family, even Ryan, wouldn't make this up," I said. Even though I wasn't trying to make her feel suspicious, she was *so* suspicious.

She had to get off the phone but agreed to talk again. She wanted a few days to think. I'm sure her head was spinning. In the meantime, I did my research for Eddie's work phone number as I learned he worked for the local train depot and was given his direct work telephone number. Apparently, Tina did not want to believe that she might have another sister but after communicating, she seemed to go along with the story for the sake of the moment.

After a couple more phone calls with Tina, I explained that I really wanted to call Eddie and she gave me his work number which matched my own research. She was very reluctant, understandably, but I always tried to reassure her I was who I said I was. Tina told me later that her mother had asked who I was, and she told her simply that I was Ryan's cousin from Connecticut. That was true, and an easy out.

It took me another few days to work up the courage to call Eddie. I would pace at night wondering when I should just bite the bullet and call. I was overthinking everything in life then. I wondered if he had thought about me and/or where I was over the years.

When I finally decided to pick up the phone to call him, I was shaking like I did when I was 15 calling for Sharon. *Déjà vu.*

It was around 6:00 p.m. in October one evening when I decided to finally pick up the phone.

Ring. Ring. Ring.

Eddie actually answered the phone.

"Hi, I'm looking for Ed, Ed Pyke" I choked the words out.

"Yea, yea, that's me" he would say excitedly fast.

"Do you remember Sharon?" I asked quietly.

There were a few seconds of silence.

"Yea, yea, I do," he sounded quizzical.

"My name is Michelle, Sharon's daughter, and your daughter." I explained who I was.

A long pause.

"I've been waiting for this call for a long time." He absolutely acknowledged me.

He thought I had been raised in Pennsylvania or somewhere else. It was a shock to say the least, but he said all the right things, explaining that I have two sisters who would LOVE to have another sister and that his wife would have to know. I never mentioned that I had been speaking to Tina, but I had planned to tell him. I told him he did not need to cause an upheaval within his family. I wanted to take things slow with him.

Turns out he really did live one town over from Kahnawake throughout all these years and still lives there today. He told me the same story Sharon had told me when he heard I was born. He said that he was very upset that he had lost a daughter and when he looked at pictures of his two girls in his home now, he realized there should have been three. That was his story at the time.

He again reiterated that he should tell his wife and I again said that if he felt he should, then by all means, but if it was going to upset her then don't. It wasn't like I needed anything. I was married, working and had a family. Basically, I felt like I was finally living the so-called all-American dream.

I sent him a letter to his work address after talking a few times on the phone and included some photos of myself and my family. Simply put, after all these years, all I needed was to see the face of the man who was my biological father. I needed to see if there was a resemblance between us.

A couple of weeks later I made the mistake of telling Tina that her father wanted to tell her mother. She went off the rails screaming into the phone calling Eddie a stupid man.

"What?! Stupid man! Stupid man! My mother will go absolutely crazy!" She tore into me during a follow-up phone call.

I tried to reassure her that I told him he didn't have to tell her mom. She didn't trust the situation. Unfortunately, Tina then called Eddie and let him know that she knew what was going on. This of course angered him because I did not tell him how I found him even though I planned to. I wasn't ready. I wanted things to be easy but that would not be. I realized it never would have been the right time to tell him.

After Tina spoke to him, I called him again that night and profusely apologized for not telling him I had been in contact with Tina first. I explained how it all came to be. He seemed to grunt at me but then turned things around and within a split second became jovial again.

"Don't worry about anything. We'll still meet up," he said.
"Are you sure?" I wasn't quite sure about him.

I think this is where he started to set up in his mind how things were going to go and unbeknownst to me it wasn't going to be in my favor.

We made arrangements to meet. Sharon reluctantly agreed to let me meet him at her house. I was grateful for that, although I knew she was uncomfortable with the idea of seeing him again after all this time.

In November 1999, my family and I drove up to Canada arriving at Sharon's house early in the afternoon. My husband,

Mike, had gone to get gas after we arrived. Eddie was driving through Kahnawake when he noticed our Durango with CT license plates at the gas station and followed it. We described our vehicles at the time we planned the meeting. Mike came into the house first and told me Eddie was in the driveway. Sharon was in the bathroom brushing her teeth and my six-year-old son was laying down on the sofa after our long drive. I was frozen standing in the kitchen, not sure I could move or even utter words. My heart was pounding. I watched Eddie come up the stairs and I put my hands to my face and started crying. We hugged tightly and he seemed thrilled. Looking at him was like looking in the mirror. I looked so much like him in so many ways. The same facial features, the same skin tone, the same eyes, lips and nose, even the same brown hair. It was uncanny. Biologically, I was *his* daughter.

We sat down for a bit and talked. I apologized again for contacting Tina explaining that it was my only resource to find him. He said it was 'water under the bridge now' patting my arm – but was it really?

Sharon finally came out to greet Eddie – toothbrush in her mouth laughing nervously. Eddie hugged her too. At that moment, it was sort of surreal having both biological parents in the same room after so many years. We sat down across from each other at the kitchen table. My prayers had been answered, I had been able to put both biological parents together if even for a short time. I had the closure I needed. Or so I thought. Sharon was a bundle of nerves, but I gave her a gift to help her with her uneasiness. It was a beautiful gold Mother and two Children pendant. She cried and had to leave the room for a moment to compose herself. Eddie seemed rather emotional too. I gave him a CD with the song "Somewhere Out There" from the film *An American Tail* about a mouse who had lost his family but reunited with them again.

"I don't a have a disc player in my truck, but I'll have to take my wife's car for a spin and give it a listen." He said.

I think he knew the song had a special meaning for me.

Sharon came back into the kitchen, grabbed a few beers for us although Eddie declined to have a drink because he had to go to work. I was too nervous to even think about having a beer. I simply found myself staring at this man. My father. We began filling in the blanks of the last thirty years. He was of English and Scottish descent. I asked about any family medical issues I should be aware of. He assured me that there really were no medical issues to be concerned with other than one of his relatives that suffered a heart attack many years before.

I quickly scooted out to the living room to grab my camera and took my son's hand to escort him into the kitchen with me.

"Come meet your grandfather." I said excitedly although Ray didn't seem to grasp the importance.
"Okay everyone, let's take some pictures." Everyone stood up to pose for a group photo. Mike held the camera and snapped away.

It was nice having a picture taken with my birth parents. It was nice to have a photo of my son with his biological grandfather. Looking at the two of them, wow! They looked alike too. The resemblance was crazy.

Shortly after, Tina showed up with a little boy. He was her son, Owen, from a previous relationship. She was still dating my cousin, Ryan, at this time. Owen immediately jumped up on Eddie's lap. I smiled as I watched their loving connection. I dreamed Ray would someday bond with his grandfather also.

About an hour later, Eddie, Tina and Owen left, and I collapsed on the sofa with a big sigh. I was emotionally exhausted. It was still all surreal to me. Did this just happen?

"Well?" Sharon wondered out loud.

I had no words. "Let me process this," was all I could say.

As for the rest of the weekend, Eddie came over each day before going to work in the afternoons at the local railroad depot. We talked a lot. Some of the conversations I can't even recall but remember sitting there having coffee. I couldn't help but stare at him. He and my husband would talk about their passion for cars and sometimes Eddie would challenge my husband about specific details of cars, and Mike would come right back with the correct answers. Eddie was taken aback a bit because Mike actually seemed to know more than he was given credit for as far as cars and mechanics went. Maybe it was a guy thing.

Tina also dropped by to see me throughout the weekend, which I thought was nice. I loved having another sister. We even shared lunch together one day in Montreal. We shared some small talk and a few laughs, but I sensed she was still a bit uneasy. So was I. Seeing her, like my father, was like looking in the mirror. Although she was blonde and blue eyed and I was brunette with brown eyes, we had the same face. It was mind boggling. We took more pictures to preserve our time together. Pictures don't lie.

Eddie was still on the notion that he was going to tell his wife and said this in front of Tina. I told them both that he didn't have to do this, pointing out, I don't need anything and the last thing I wanted to do was upset anyone. Eddie would have to think about it.

The evening before I left, there was another moment when Eddie said something out of line, disguised in sarcasm, but it really wasn't funny to me. "You know, there's so much confusion on the reservation about Fathers' Day." He looked right at Sharon. I thought that was a rude jab at her, but she took it in stride.

"You know she's yours!" She snapped back at him. He didn't respond, just sat quietly. Sharon had put Eddie in his place.

At the end of the evening as he left, we walked outside to say our good-byes.

"Call me when you get back, ok?" he looked at me with tears.

"Sure, I'll call you." I promised. It felt nice that he seemed concerned.

"You know, I'm really sorry about talking to Tina first, but if I didn't, I wouldn't have known where you were and believe me, I searched for a long time." I was sincere.

"Well, it all makes sense, and you know I'll have to tell my wife something," he said. I knew it made him uncomfortable.

"You don't have to Eddie. There's nothing I need or want, seriously. Don't upset anyone," I said.

"It'll be fine. You'll be a part of our family and you'll come to our cabin in Quebec for Christmas." He went on and on as if I was going to be a big part of his family. I was hopeful but not sure it would become real. Happy endings were not typically in the cards for me.

Eddie made all sorts of promises that I would be a part of his family. He told my son, his grandson, that he would take him fishing and that he couldn't wait to have us in his life.

Because of the stories I had heard about his wife, I wondered if that was a good idea. I knew Tina did not think it would ever fly with her mother and my gut was telling me the same thing. Even my husband said we needed to be careful. Mike did not trust Eddie. He had a sense that he was not totally sincere and may be just a player. My mind turned back to my grandmother's letter to me telling me that she did not want me to find him. She knew I would get hurt. But Eddie was my biological father. I desperately hoped we would continue our father/daughter relationship in the future.

After we left that weekend to go home, I was very emotional during the six-hour ride. My heart was full yet unsure about Eddie. Should I really trust him?

Once I was back home, Eddie and I spoke again on the phone. He had asked me to write Sandy, his wife, a letter, to which I did and faxed to him for approval, and he thought it was "beautiful." I was hopeful.

Fast forward a few weeks after I sent the letter, I got a call from Sandy. I could see the Caller ID had indicated their last name and I just knew it was her. Why was I nervous all of a sudden?

"Hello?" I answered.

"Michelle?" that familiar voice of Sandy's sounded when I first called Tina

"This is Sandy. I received your letter," she didn't sound very warm.

"Oh good, I'm so glad you received it." I was polite and calm.

"Glad?! What do you mean glad?!" She roared.

"Glad that hopefully things are ok?" I did not understand her hostility at the moment.

"When I showed Eddie the letter, he was off the walls!" she said.

"I don't understand, he wanted me to write you a letter and he approved it." I explained in matter of fact.

"What do you mean he approved of it? He told me that he told you to get out of his life!" She was hoppin' mad!

"Um, no…he told me he wanted me to be a part of your family and I told him, only if you agreed." I proceeded to tell her.

"You think he's going to be a father to you now? You think he's going to be your son's grandfather?" I think she was ready to come through the phone.

154

"Sandy, he's an adult, I think he can make his own decisions!" I snapped back.

"Someone's bullshitting me here!" She accused.

"It's not me, Sandy!" I stood firm in reply.

In the background, Mike was yelling at me to hang up the phone. Sandy had already slammed the phone down. But it wasn't long before the phone rang again and this time, Sandy had Eddie on the phone too.

"Hello…" I answered angrily.

"Eddie…did you tell Michelle to write me this letter?!" She confronted him. She apparently had conferenced him in on another line from his work.

"Um….err…. ladies, I have to work." Eddie squirreled his way out of the conversation and hung up the phone leaving Sandy and I hanging.

"Sandy, I'm not lying to you." I think she knew full well it wasn't me who was lying but chose not to hear me.

"Well, did you know he told us you were harassing him by calling him several times a day?!" That couldn't have been further from the truth.

"Excuse me? No, no…I never did that. We would plan the calls when he was available and that's how we arranged things." I was fit to be tied. Could it be that my 'father' was now lying about everything?

"He'll never be your father!" She snapped.

"It's up to him" I knew she would never allow it. I also knew she would never let her daughters have any sort of relationship with me.

I told her about the letters and photos I sent to Eddie and Tina. Apparently, Eddie lied to her saying I never sent him any letter with photos. Wow! I was amused. I told her I would send her a copy of everything I had sent him if she didn't believe me. I never did. I think she knew deep down that I was telling the truth. I didn't want to further disrupt their family. At this point,

I was devastated that my dream of a father/daughter relationship would never come to be. My grandmother was right.

I told Sandy that Eddie and I met at Sharon's. I wasn't holding the truth back any longer. I wasn't trying to save feelings anymore. Once Eddie learned that I told Sandy the truth, Eddie called me back, again on a three-way call with her, screaming at me to lose his phone number, never to call him again. I confronted him with all that said to me and his response was, he was 'saving feelings.'

Lo and behold, no big surprise, it turns out Eddie made me out to be huge monster. Tina, his daughter, was of no help and stayed quiet through it all. She backed up Eddie's every last word. I think she did it for the sake of her mother even though she knew the truth. Tina knew when she met me in person that I wasn't a monster whatsoever. She knew and heard what I said. She knew and heard me tell Eddie he didn't have to say anything. I had no plans of doing anyone any harm. But I would be forced to deal with whatever he decided to do. Basically, we needed to let the chips fall wherever they fell. I didn't expect them to fall so hard. Nothing ever came easy in my life; rejection is still a hard pill to swallow.

Apparently, Eddie told Sandy that I 'forced him' to meet me. Nothing could have been further from the truth. He came to meet me on his own without a gun to his head. I wish Tina had taken a stand but if she went against her parents, I'm sure there would have been hell to pay. I figured that is why Tina didn't dare say or do anything. Tina and her sister, Val, had their hands tied and refused to ever have anything to do with me. That makes me sad even today. Still though, I hope that one day we may come together.

Several days after all the phone calls, Tina told Ryan that her mother had asked me for a DNA test, and that I had refused. WHAT?! Sharon called me and asked me if this was true. That was the last straw! I was angry. It was a lie. I said I would have gladly given vials of blood had I actually been asked. I still would today. It's not like Eddie ever denied that I was his daughter. I thought about calling Sandy back and confronting her, but that would have gotten me nowhere. Sandy knows the truth.

Interestingly, I think Sandy is reminded of me every so often with her younger daughter Tina's son from another native of Kahnawake. I always wondered if Sandy thought of me when she saw her grandson's native family. Karma. To be quite honest, it is my belief Sandy knew I was born from the start but chose to ignore and forget about it all along until I came back. It really doesn't take long for news to get around up there.

After all this, I was filled with anxiety and grief for quite a while. Sleep was not my friend. It took me a long time to get myself back to a better place about my adoption.

In the back of my mind, I was hoping that Eddie and I could have a relationship but instead I ended up writing a letter to Eddie and faxing it, calling him a coward, a liar and I'm sure a few other expletives telling him that things could've have been a whole lot easier if he wasn't such a douchebag. I reminded him that he never had to tell his wife. That was his decision. There was nothing I needed or wanted from him. Nothing. As far as I was concerned after all that, my one and only 'real' father, was Tom.

As for my half-sisters, Tina and Val, I wished they hadn't been given such an illusion of me being so horrible. I'm sure they know deep down that I am not evil. Tina especially knew that. It was always my dream to have sisters. It was my hope that we could have a relationship as the years went on but that was not to be thanks to their parents. A few years later when Myspace and Facebook came out, I reached out to Tina and Val, but it was to no avail. They ignored my messages.

I'll never forget Eddie's lies or Sandy's nasty accusations and nasty comments of me wanting money, trying to ruin a family, that he'll never be my father, and he would never be my son's grandfather. I was stunned. No words. I didn't want anything from that family other than Eddie's acknowledgment.

I never saw or heard from Eddie again. I'm sure however he thinks about this every day, and he will die with this on his conscience. I wonder if Eddie ever genuinely felt sorry about it all. I'll never know. I got what I wanted though. I was finally able to put a face to the man that made me. I think about that letter my grandmother had written me, warning me about Eddie. She was so right about the hurt I would experience but I had to find out for myself.

Who Am I? I am Tom's daughter.

Update: In 2020, I received a message on a DNA website from a woman who believed we were related, and that Eddie was also her father. She described a relationship between her mother and a truck driver from Canada, having the same name. She described Eddie to a perfect match. I told her I wouldn't even bother to contact him because it would not be pleasant but then again, she may have a better reception than I got. It absolutely would not surprise me that Eddie may have more children out there somewhere. He was charming and a player. As of this writing, I do not know if this woman ever contacted him. Nor have I heard from her since. Whatever happened or didn't happen, it's on Eddie.

CHAPTER 12 – LEA'S FINAL YEARS
2001 - 2006

2001

Lea's obvious mental illness along with other health struggle such as diabetes, had become increasingly worse. Her hoarding tendencies seemed to magnify after I had moved out of her house some seventeen years before. She could never afford upkeep in or out of the house. Both her physical and mental health declined to the point she couldn't or refused to clean herself; using the kitchen chair she sat on sometimes as a toilet while watching television. It became a house of horrors.

This is very hard for me to write because it brings the pain back. I know if Lea were still here, she would feel that same pain. There are mixed emotions.

Our relationship was always rocky but after I became an adult, it was even more so. After I married Mike, things had started to take a good turn in the relationship, but it didn't last forever. I knew so little about mental illness at the time. It was as if she knew she couldn't hurt me physically, but she would find other ways throughout time.

During those good years, we would go shopping and have lunch. I would help her at the flea markets occasionally. She would join Mike and I on the occasional day trip or out for dinner. She would also spend time with our son but only under careful watch.

On the days when it was just she and I alone, we would sometimes have conversations about my adoption and how it affected me. She would tell me that she probably should have told me when I was younger. She believed I wouldn't have had all the issues I did growing up. Deep in my mind, however I felt it would have made things worse.

"Mom, why didn't you ever tell me I was adopted before I found out by Rita?" I would ask knowing that her answer would not soothe me.

"I don't know. I probably should have told you when you were younger. You might have had a better handle on things." she hurried her answer, "I was going to wait until you were eighteen as I said before. I thought you would have handled it better then, but I know now that was not a good idea." She just wanted to drop the conversation knowing that no matter what she said, it would not redeem her.

"Mom, I think the truth from the beginning probably would have been best." That was it; I dropped it. There really was no reason to keep bringing it up. I was not going to feel any comfort.

After that, we never really talked much more about my 'adoption fiasco' as I knew it would never be put to rest in my mind or hers. I decided to just move on and accept that my relationship with Lea would be what it was, good and bad.

By the time my son was in elementary school, I noticed Lea's behavior changing. While she's always demonstrated bouts of anger toward me, she seemed to be getting noticeably forgetful. It seemed evident that I needed to be alert around her and protect myself emotionally. Without realizing it, I started to distance myself.

One Saturday, she decided she was going to attend a local rummage sale at a Church nearby my mother in law's house. Unbeknownst to us, instead of going to that rummage sale, Lea decided to pay a visit to my mother-in-law, Barbara's house, instead. Mike, Ray, and I were out and about running errands and grabbing a bite to eat so we had no idea Lea had gone over there unannounced. If anything, my mother-in-law expected a phone call before people just went over to visit.

Barbara was obviously surprised to see Lea at the door and wondered if something had happened. Apparently, Lea came to Barbara's house to search for things that might belong to her. After all these years, she still hung on to the belief that I had stolen property from her as a teenager and hid them at Barbara's. Lea demanded that Barbara open her basement door and garage, but Barbara refused to do so explaining that she wanted to call us to come over first. She tried calling us several times but was only able to leave us messages. Remember this was before the cell era.

"Mike, it's Mom. Lea is over here, and I was hoping you and Michelle could come over," She pleaded on the answering machine. "She thinks Michelle brought some of her personal belongings over here," she went on, "alright, call me back." Barbara called several times.

Mike had listened to messages as I was still outside with our son just playing frisbee. He came outside with a look on his face that was disturbing and angry.

"My mom called. Your mother is over there causing problems." He seemed pissed.
"What problems?" I couldn't wait to hear this. My stomach jumped into knots.
"She's looking around my mother's house for stuff you supposedly brought over there. I'm heading over there now." He started to get in the car.

"Hold on, let me call your mom back quickly!" I flew into the house picking up the phone.

161

"Barbara, what's going on?!" I was out of breath.

"Your mother was here but she left once Mike called to say he was coming over." I think Lea got nervous and didn't want to deal with Mike or me.

Barbara was relieved I called her but she still seemed offended that Lea had accused her of hiding stolen property. I couldn't blame Barbara. I was raging all of a sudden.

"Oh my God, I hope you know that this isn't true. I'm afraid she's not well. Ok, I will take care of this. Barbara, I'm so sorry she did that to you. This isn't the first time she pulled something sneaky like this. She's accused me of crazy things all my life. She's obviously the one who's crazy!"

Barbara didn't seem surprised given the fact she tried so many times to reach out to Lea many times rebuffing Barbara's calls or friendship at times, because of me.

I waited to make sure Lea was home before I called her. Afterall, she had driven 25 miles out of her way to cause problems.

I actually didn't even want to talk to her when I was dialing her number. My walls were up, and I felt ready to blast her.

"Hello!" she answered in a nasty tone.

"Mom! What is going on?" I asked, trying so hard not to lose my cool.

"You know!" She snapped.

"Really, I don't. Why did you go over to Barbara's like that? She doesn't like it when people just show up and she certainly doesn't like to be accused of hiding things from the lies you tell yourself!"

"So?" She had an evil tone to her voice.

I was fit to be tied. Mike was in the background telling me to just hang up. He was done with her, and his family would be done with her. He wasn't playing games.

"I just wanted to see Barbara," she lied.
"You started to go through her house! You demanded she open her basement door and garage door – WHY?" I started yelling now.
"So what? You stole stuff from my house! I watched you go in my house and come out of it with stuff"
"What STUFF?" I screamed.
"You know what stuff!" She screamed.
I wasn't about to go around in circles with her.
"Mom, please, let's go through what I stole from you? I don't have a key to your house, so how would I even get in?"
"You didn't use a key! You removed the window pane from the back door!" Wow!

WHAT?! That was it! I was silent. I felt she had lost her mind at that moment and my memories started flooding back to when I was in elementary school and the house had been "broken into" where someone had taken the window pane out of the back door to gain entry.

"Mom, I never stole anything from you." I was nauseous.

Suddenly, I felt the need to protect everyone around me, not just myself. I knew I had to just cut her off from my life and everyone in it.

"Mom, you can't keep doing this to me. I don't think we should talk for a while. I never stole anything from you and you know it!"

"Yes, you did!" She screamed and slammed her phone down.

I was trembling. My blood pressure felt like it was going through the roof. I knew things were not going to get better from here. All the good that we had finally managed was lost. She really seemed to hate me. Again.

I don't know what bothered me more, Lea thinking she could intrude on my family like this or that she thought she could hurt me anytime she wanted to. I wanted to believe things had been going well for the last few years but apparently, she wanted to cause an upheaval in the balance I thought I finally obtained.

What I started to realize was that her mental health was more unstable than ever but there was nothing I could do about it. I say this only because a few days later Lea called, and I let Mike answer the phone. I had had enough.

"Hello?" He was cordial.

"Mike? I thought you were going to come over to move boxes for me down to my basement?" She was cheerful to him. It was like night and day. It was like she completely forgot about the situation.

"I never said that, and you didn't ask. No, I'm not coming over there." He waited for her reply. There was none. She hung up the phone.

I can't say we were shocked. We were getting used to her erratic behavior and increased forgetfulness.

After that, all seemed quiet for a while. We didn't hear from her, and nobody within her extended family ever reached out. I felt like an outcast on some level, but I didn't worry about it as I had things to do and my own family to take care of. I still had a connection with my birth family at the time. That was enough for me, then.

Who Am I? I am a lost daughter to an adoptive mother.

Summer 2002

The next time I would have to have contact with Lea was when Tom's two older children, David, and Denise, called me because they wanted to visit me and were hoping to also meet with Lea to get some clarity about Tom. I explained that she was not well and that I hadn't spoken to her in several months. I shared with them some of the difficulties I had been having with Lea. My sister, Denise thought perhaps she could help me mend things with her but I stopped her,

"Denise, don't even bother. Her mental state has changed since the last time you met her years ago. I've been dealing with her all my life and she's never going to change."

Despite my warning, both Denise and David still insisted on coming to Connecticut to see us. Even if their encounter with Lea backfired, both Denise and I were still excited to be meeting our brother for the very first time.

Just a few weeks later, both David and Denise traveled to Connecticut. David took a bus from his home Maine and Denise took the train from her home in Baltimore. Mike cleaned the house and prepared for their stay. Denise arrived first. We were sipping coffee together as David's taxi dropped him off from the bus station. He arrived early. We heard his very distinct low toned voice. We looked out the window. Our brother was short, stout, and bald. Not what we were expecting. The last photo I saw of him was when he was about 16 years old. He was now in his early 50s. We excitedly ran out to greet him in the driveway. He gave us the biggest bear hug. We were overjoyed. I couldn't believe we were finally all together after all these years. I didn't even know I had a brother from my adoptive family until Denise told me about David when she first visited me about 10 years. It would take us several years of internet searches, phone calls and research to locate him in Maine. David had been recently married at the time. He and his wife, Marlene, didn't have any children.

Mike greeted us inside with Ray who was now nine years old. Although a bit shy, I think Ray was excited to meet his new aunt and uncle. After a bit of chit chat and a pot roast dinner I had prepared for them, they asked when they could meet Lea.

I took a deep sigh. I knew I had to bite the bullet and reach out to Lea. It had been a long time, but how bad could it be? I picked up the phone.

"Hello?"

"Mom?"

"What the HELL do you want you thief!" She greeted me.

"Mom, please stop – I'm calling you because David and Denise are here, and they would like to see you?" I tried to explain.

"I don't need to see them," She hissed.

"You know Mom, they didn't do anything wrong, and they just want answers about Daddy (Tom)" I tried to plead on their behalf.

"What answers?" Oh, she was so defiant. I just about gave up.

"Well fine, if they want to see me, they can't come to my house. We'll have to go somewhere else!"

"Ok – fine. How about I come pick you up and take you to the restaurant down the road from you? Ok?" I just didn't care at this point.

"Ok." Click. I couldn't even finish giving her the date knowing I would have to call her again.

She picked up the phone in silence.

"Mom, let's do Tuesday for our plan, ok?" I pleaded. I knew I would never do this again. I was so sick of her treatment. She hung up the phone, again. I sighed.

My brother and sister, David and Denise, Mike, Ray, and I had a very nice visit. I showed them around my town. We also took a day to see the house that Tom lived in before he died, and we made a trip to the cemetery where he was buried and laid fresh flowers. We took photos of all three of our shadows overlooking Tom's headstone. It turned very tearful when we all realized that we never had the chance to be together when our father was alive. I know he would have loved that. The three of us locked arms as we gazed at his headstone in silence. We were very happy that we had each other now.

The next day, I had to drop them off at the restaurant we chose and pick up Lea to bring her there. It was a daunting day. My stomach was jumping again. I was praying Lea would behave. I knew I was not going to be welcome at the table and told David and Denise I would wait outside while they talked.

I knocked on her door loudly enough so she would know I was there. She came out with a glare on her face.

"Why are YOU here?!" She screamed at me. She forgot.
"Mom, stop, please. David and Denise are waiting for you down at the restaurant," I said calmly.
"Oh…I thought that was yesterday." She went back in to get her pocketbook. Oh, how I wanted to just leave her where I found her, but I couldn't let David or Denise down. We drove in silence.

She went into the restaurant, and I parked in a corner parking space and waited. About a half-hour later I saw my sister, Denise, come out looking for me. She could barely walk with her bad knees, so I drove up to her. She wanted me to come in. She wanted to bring peace to us. I told her I knew Lea did not want me to come in. She took my hand, asked me to turn off the car and to just walk with her and promised me everything would be alright. I loved her for that. Denise is a loving sister.

I went in with her and sat down next to Lea. Lea seemed to be ok for the moment. David was asking questions about Tom.

"Lea, do I look like Dad?" David would ask.

"You do." she would answer nicely.

"Does he really?" I mumbled - assuming she didn't want me to talk.

"Yes, he does." Lea turned and actually smiled at me. I almost fell off my seat when she answered me nicely.

They finished their coffee and ice cream and we all headed back to her house to drop her off. I had David and Denise walk in the field towards the reservoir while I spoke with Lea for a moment.

"I hope you enjoyed seeing them again." I was genuine. She hadn't seen David since he was a teenager, and last saw Denise in 1992 when she came to Connecticut for the first time to meet us.

"I did. I told them about what you did!" She looked proud.

"Of course, you did Mom. But you know I didn't do anything and I've proven that!" How much more could I plead with her?

"I watched you break into my house and come back out with boxes." Yep. Here we go again.

"Mom – I have no time to drive from my town to yours and you know that!" She had tears in her eyes. This was rare. The last time I saw tears was when the 'adoption bombshell' happened.

She left to go into the house. There was nothing more I could say and that was the last of our communication again for a while.

I caught up with David and Denise in the field and asked them if my mother had said anything about what I told them, and they looked at me and said Lea hadn't said anything. They both came to the conclusion that Lea wasn't well, but she was able to provide some answers to their questions about our father, Tom. I think they felt better about their own situations. I was glad for them. Of course, there were always questions that loomed and some would never be answered. They seemed at peace with what they received from Lea.

The next morning, Mike and I drove my brother and sister to the bus/train station in Hartford to see them off. I was sad to see them go. It was the first time in my life I had two of my siblings together with me even if just for a short time. We all promised that we would keep in touch with each other, however, other than a few phone calls, our communication started waning. Three siblings, three secrets, three decades to come together because of Lea, the secret holder. Denise went home to Maryland, to resume her life with her husband, Tom, and their children and grandchildren. Our older brother, David, went home to his bride, Marlene, in Maine and continued his quiet life there in the woods as a furniture builder. Life went on.

UPDATE - In 2020, my brother David passed away suddenly. Other than an occasional phone call, I regret not having kept in touch as much as we should since seeing each other for the last time in 2002. My sister, Denise, my brother, David and I were thankful we had at least found each other despite Lea, the secret keeper, preventing us from knowing each other. Three siblings, three secrets, and three decades to come together but we prevailed. Through the pain of David's death, I gained a precious friend, Kathy. I met her at David's memorial service. She had been one of David's lifelong friends. We have remained in touch, and I am grateful to have her in my life. My sister, Denise and I are still in touch and I am grateful for that too..

Downhill from there ...

It would be a few more months before I would have contact again with Lea. I had been working full-time as a legal professional and spending all my free time with my family. I didn't have time for anything else but that was ok with me. A drama free life was a welcome respite, at least for a while.

One morning as I arrived at work, Mike called to tell me that a police officer in Lea's town had called and wanted me to call him back. I was a bit surprised but wondered if something had happened to her. So, I went home for lunch that day to listen to the message.

"Hello, this is Detective Smith of the Police Department. I have a few concerns regarding your mother, Lea. Please call me at your earliest convenience."

Great, now what? I called him back only to leave him a message on his voice mail and gave him my work number to reach me as I was headed back to office. My stomach was churning. I honestly believe that I was dealing with PTSD.

While back at work, I had trouble concentrating and waited with angst for this detective's call back. It didn't come that day and it kept me up that night. My poor husband knew this was really bothering me and he tried to calm me down, but it just wasn't helping. Lea was just going to be a problem and would stop at nothing to try and hurt me. I felt like I was public enemy number one.

As I went to work the next day, I finally received the detective's call back.

"Hi Michelle, this is Officer Smith. I'm sorry I couldn't return your call yesterday, I was out on another matter," He was very nice.
"Oh, that's ok, I know how busy your job can be." I reciprocated his cordialness.

"So, your mother, Lea, has been coming to the station here for the last several months. She believes you have been breaking into her home and stealing several items," he sighed.

"You know that's not true at all. I haven't seen her in months and this fictitious story has been told since I was a teenager." I answered.

"We know it's not true. We realize there are issues here and when we questioned her about the items taken, she could not give us answers." Apparently, she would not even allow the officer into her home. When Officer Smith asked for Lea's permission to investigate her property, she flat out refused. *Déjà vu!* Again. I was immediately brought back to when I was removed from her house all those years ago.

"Thank you for letting me know this. I'm sure you realize it's all in her head. She has problems." I explained.

"I totally understand Michelle. I have to tell you too that when her car was parked at the station, we noticed that it was unregistered, without insurance, and she is an unlicensed driver. We had it towed from our parking lot and gave her a warning regarding these issues. She is not allowed to drive any vehicles in her driveway until she resolves this," he explained. Since he had suspected, she was going to become problematic he told me he had investigated my whereabouts to at least inform me of what was going on.

"Oh, I'm not surprised. She has always done this. She does not like to follow the rules." I explained that this had gone on for years and I explained our relationship or lack thereof.

"Very interesting," he said. "Ok, I also have made a referral to the Department of Social Services because I don't believe she is well, and it looks like she needs some help." He gave me the direct phone number of the social worker that I needed to call. Although I always suspected my mother had mental illness, it felt like our family secret was finally exposed. My head began to hurt. I was numb.

He continued, "We'll keep this report on file should your mother come back, and I will let her know that we spoke with you and we do not believe you are committing any crimes nor have any intention to do so. I'll send you a copy." He was generous in his response, and I thanked him for his time.

Surprisingly, I was genuinely concerned about Lea's well-being, but it all had to stop. I needed to stand up for myself. I knew getting Lea professional help would be the first step albeit not an easy one.

I called the social worker at Department of Social Services (DSS) next. I gave him a synopsis of our relationship. DSS also did not believe the allegations Lea was asserting against me. They knew she needed help, and I was the only family member to come forward. The social worker suggested placing her in an assisted living home.

The only other family member who came around to see her was her brother, my uncle, Paul, but he would not speak to me about anything because of all the lies Lea told him about me. He had no idea how unstable she really was. I think he blamed me.

From there, everything about Lea's life became a blur. She was getting older. She was forgetting to pay her bills. She wasn't allowed to drive. She would walk everywhere. When it became evident that she could not even do that anymore she would ask complete strangers to give her rides. Her health was declining rapidly. Despite everything, Uncle Paul still refused to acknowledge it.

DSS asked me to become her conservator / power of attorney and take over her affairs as it would be better "if a family member" took care of her. Hmmm. I realized that I was the only one who would be able to handle her. Nobody else in Lea's family ever stepped up to help her that I knew of. Her brother, Paul, just watched from the sidelines. I had to legally take matters into my own hands. I was ANGRY. Angry that Lea had a family who knew she was in distress, but no one stepped in to help or visit her. I figured they believed it was somehow all my fault.

After probate applications were filed, I took on the role of conservatorship. Honestly, this was for both her sake and for my own personal reasons, even if a bit selfish (I wanted access to the house to find my baby pictures and any other personal items.) After I was appointed, I received the paperwork to add my name to her one bank account as Conservator. One bank employee who I remembered giving me lollipops as a little girl, refused to add my name to the bank account. She refused to believe my mother would be a problem and just glared at me. I was mortified but realized, again, mother dear, had put the "thief bug" in her ear too. I was frustrated.

A few days later, Mom's social security check went directly into her account. I had sent checks on her account to pay her utilities and legal fees with that. Even after Lea and I had a serious discussion about this, and she seemed to understand what I was saying, she still walked down to the bank and withdrew every last penny from her bank account. I noticed it right away via the online banking website. BIG PROBLEM! Now, the checks I sent would not clear. I had a bad feeling she would do this. I had to fight with Lea to get most of the cash back. It cost me time away from my job, gasoline for the drive to her house, mental stress from arguing with her some more, and finally the frustration of having to go back to the bank to finally add my name as conservator on that account.

This time, I refused to see the bank employee and demanded to consult with the bank manager, who immediately took care of what should have been done in the first place. He said that he would speak to the employee. I never saw her in that branch again.

From there, my relationship with Lea was like a rollercoaster, uphill and downhill. Lea was getting worse. Her doctor was concerned because she did not want to take her diabetic medication and things were just deteriorating for her at home, which was still a hoarding nightmare. One time I was there to check on her and noted she would use the chair she sat on as a toilet and didn't realize it. She hadn't done laundry for months and her place just reeked of cigarettes, urine, and feces.

She would call me constantly, sometimes very late at night or at 3:00 in the morning, telling me she needed things right away. Things like cigarettes and newspapers. I would tell her that I couldn't bring these things right away. She would get so agitated that I sometimes caved to get her what she wanted. I most often pleaded with her to wait until I got out of work the next day, but she had no patience.

The phone would ring, and I knew it would be Lea because of the time.

"Hello?"

"Michelle?" She questioned not thinking it was me.

"Yes mom, what do you need? It's late."

"Oh...I thought it was one of the other girls you lived with." She was in another time warp back when I lived in foster care.

"No Mom, I've been married for a while now. Do you remember Mike and your grandson, Raymond?"

"I've never met Raymond." Here we go. The hairs on the back of my neck stood up. There was no point in trying to convince her otherwise.

"Mom, do you need something? I need to go to bed soon because I have to work tomorrow," I would try to explain.

"I need a carton of cigarettes and milk." She was agitated and probably just looking for an excuse for me to go there. She didn't have a refrigerator, only a Styrofoam cooler that was probably filled with rotten food.

"Mom, I'll bring them to you after work tomorrow, ok?" I just wanted to go to bed.

"Oh boy! Oh boy!" She was very agitated again. "I really need them now." she cried.

"Mom, I'm four towns away from you. It would take me at least a half-hour to get out there and it's very late at night. How about you go to bed?" I pleaded.

"Oh boy! Oh boy!" She wouldn't stop.

"Mom, can you try to wait until tomorrow night please?"

"I really need them now!" It was 11:00 at night.

"Fine – I'll come out now." I caved. I felt like I didn't have a choice and I didn't want her calling me all night.

"Oh good!" She was like a kid on Christmas morning.

This happened almost every week. My husband was not thrilled. Lea was a master manipulator.

One night after bringing her things that she absolutely had to have, I noticed she could barely walk. When I asked her what was going on, she looked so ill that I knew I was going to have to take her to the hospital at that moment. She bent down and lifted her dirty sweat-pant leg up and I nearly fell over! The stench was overpowering! She had a huge diabetic open wound on her lower leg that looked so deep and grossly infected. I told her she needed to get her coat and we needed to get to the ER. I figured they would admit her, and I felt that would be a good thing as I could then get her into an assisted living place where she would be bathed, fed, and looked after properly. After being at the ER for several hours, the doctors knew I wanted to get her admitted. Surprisingly, they decided not to admit her after all the tests. They discharged her with a prescription for antibiotics. She needed to be admitted. I assumed they knew, but shockingly, for some reason, they refused. I was furious. As her daughter and legal conservator, I knew what she needed. I know the doctors and nurses knew it too. So, I dropped her off at home and ran to the local CVS to pick-up her prescription. I didn't get home until 3 or 4 a.m. I didn't sleep at all. I still needed to go to work and had to make several emergent calls to DSS and her doctor's office that morning.

I walked into work like a zombie and went into the office conference room to make the necessary calls to DSS and her doctor. Her doctor immediately sent an ambulance and re-admitted Lea to another local hospital. The doctor knew Lea needed to be in assisted living and made sure it happened. It was up to me to find the place with the assistance of DSS. Luckily, I was able to find such an assisted living place. Unluckily, I was the one to have to tell Lea that she was going there. This was going to be a hard conversation to have. I went to the hospital right after work.

"Hey mom, how are you tonight?" I asked as kind and loving as possible, patting her arm.

"When am I going home?" She asked.

"Well, you need to have more medicine and then they are going to transfer you to an assisted living facility so you can get better," I fibbed and her face turned to stone.

As she lie in her hospital bed, she was not happy with me and I was subjected to more of her wrath.

"What do you mean?!" She screamed. "I'm fine! I'm going back to my house!"

"Mom you can't right now, you're too sick and we need to make things better in the house before you can go back." I told her. I was lying, but with honest intentions.

"I'm fine! You get me out of here right now!" She demanded.

"I can't right now. You're on an IV with antibiotics and you have to stay here until you are able to walk better," I lied again.

"I'm fine!"

"Ok, but you'll see, the assisted living facility will help you get better faster, ok?"

"You're no good! You're going to steal everything from me again!" She was yelling now.

Unfortunately, Lea had a roommate in the hospital who had to listen to all this. The roommate would look at me as if she understood but didn't say anything.

"Mom, I'm going to go home now, ok? I'll try to come back and see you tomorrow."

"I can take care of myself and I don't want you around!"

There was no point in reasoning. Things were happening, and I was not going to give in to her. Morally or legally, I just couldn't. While she was in the hospital, I went to the house to open the one window that she didn't have painted shut. Fresh air was desperately needed in her house.

Finally, after a week in the hospital with IV antibiotic treatment, a private ambulance brought Lea to the assisted living facility I chose. It was a beautiful, warm, and cozy place to be. I was there to meet her and take her to her room once all the paperwork was filled out and signed as her Conservator. They had given her Ativan to help her calm down when she saw me. She was very disoriented but that was normal. I knew she would be in good hands. As I got her settled and I left, I felt a tremendous weight come back on my shoulders thinking about the heavy work ahead at her house.

Winter 2002

As Lea was now residing in the assisted living home, I began the very tedious task of clearing out her house. It held so many memories that sometimes I was unable to continue, causing me to leave the house for weeks, sometimes months at a time. It was too much to bear. It triggered so many bad memories.

I had to clear out the hoard of stuff and throw away so much. I found many letters and cards from Tom's family that had come in over the years. So many well wishes and hopes to see me were dashed as Lea cut everyone off when Tom died and I didn't realize it. Why she did that, I'll never know but I felt the emotions through these letters and cards. There were also envelopes with checks that had never been cashed from former tenants. They had been stuffed in a cobweb filled dresser drawer obviously for many years.

To this day, I still think about all the correspondence I found from Tom's family. It would have been interesting if I saved everything but at the time, I was just in a rush to get it all out. Lea saved everything. This is why there were times I couldn't go back to the house for a while because of the emotions or getting physically sick due to the dust, dirt, animal feces and mold in the house. This is what I grew up in.

I ended up renting a very large storage space for the hoard that was salvageable where I would embark on becoming a huge seller on ebay. (A journey for another book).

2003-2005

In between cleaning out the house, dealing with certain legal aspects surrounding the house, working, taking care of my family and visiting Lea when I could, I was feeling exhausted and stressed.

My poor mother-in-law, Barbara, had also been placed in a nursing home just a year before Lea and when Barbara passed in 2005, it was a very hard time for our family. Barbara also had dementia probably caused by diabetes. It was a very rough time having both our mothers in homes and having two houses to clean out at the same time. This put a lot of stress on us, but we held it together as best as we could.

During this time, I saw Lea's health and memory declining rapidly. It was getting harder and harder to visit her. I knew I had put her in a good place but that was about to change once again.

While I was at work, I received a call from the director of the facility stating that Lea was falling often, and they could not continue to care for her in this condition. She would need a 24-hour care facility at this point. The thought of filling out all the paperwork again was nauseating. I kept thinking she never would have done this for me while I was in foster care. Not one iota. And yet, I was the person that knew nobody else would take care of Lea. Not even her brother, Paul.

I found a facility just up the road from where I lived at the time. I arranged for the current facility to transport her. Lea didn't understand why she had to leave and thought she would go back to her own house. She was told the house was sold and proceeded to have a total angry meltdown. In reality, the house was not sold yet. I was still cleaning it out. It took years. When I heard what Lea was told about the house, I proceeded to give the director a piece of my mind. Why would you say something like that knowing it would cause a reaction in this manner? They knew my mother. It was over and done with and I chose to just let it go because Lea wouldn't be able to understand anything due to her worsening dementia.

Once again, it was another visit to another nursing home, having to fill out paperwork and then making sure she was set for her first night there. They also had to give her Ativan to calm her down, put an alarm on her and put her in a chair that she could not get out of. My heart broke seeing her or anyone like this. It didn't seem humane.

With Lea being closer to my home, I thought it would be easier to visit but in truth, I found it harder to visit more often than I should have for so many emotional reasons. I had peace of mind that she was in a safe place.

As the months passed, Lea would decline further and rambled on about taking drives to visit her family in Massachusetts. I would just let her talk and would join her conversation about how her day was in Massachusetts. She would regale me in her adventures and say her family would never see her again. I would just nod my head.

"Hi Mom, how was your day?" I asked as I approached her in the activity room one day.
"I drove up to Massachusetts to see my cousins," she told me believing she really did this.
"Oh, did you now? How was the drive?" I played along.
"They'll never see me again! Ever!" She exclaimed.
"How come?" I would ask, just to keep up.
"They don't like that I'm married to him." she said.
"To who? Daddy?" I would ask quizzically.
"Daddy who?" She seemed confused. I was confused.
"You know, Tom, your husband? Daddy?" I tried to remind her.

She would never say another word about that conversation. I wasn't sure if she was remembering something from a long time ago.

"Did you have good weather driving to see your family?" I asked in a different way.

"They'll never see me again!" She stopped talking and started talking to her nurse who had just come in to give her some medication.

It was really a strange conversation as I had heard through the grapevine that she had been secretly married before she married Tom, but she NEVER told me about it. I never pursued the story, and I never found any paperwork while cleaning out the house. It was just one of those mysteries about Lea.

During this time that Lea was in the home, my birth mother had come to visit us for a few days. Sharon knew Lea was not well and she wanted to see her. I told her I could make no promises as to what kind of mood Lea would be in and basically just take whatever is said or done with a grain of salt. Sharon was fine with that as she understood what was going on. Before we would go see Lea, I showed Sharon around my town and introduced her to friends of ours.

One of the mornings while she was there visiting, as I was getting ready for a visit to see Lea, Sharon asked if she could come along. Sharon and Lea met approximately twelve years before, when my son, Ray, was a baby. There didn't seem to be any animosity between the two mothers. It was still surreal to me having my biological mother and my adoptive mother in the same room.

When we arrived at the nursing home, Lea was in her wheelchair in the activity room just staring out the window. As I greeted Lea and reintroduced her to Sharon, she would not turn around to say hello to Sharon, nor would she talk to me. I asked her nurse to ask if anything happened that day, and the nurse explained that Lea had suddenly just stopped talking. It had been a couple of weeks since I had visited, and I was not aware of this. It wasn't that she couldn't physically talk, she just refused to. Apparently, this is normal with dementia patients. I whispered this to Sharon, and she nodded with understanding. Sharon and I sat down with Lea and made small talk trying to pull her into the conversation, but she never acknowledged us, just staring out the window. We decided to leave, and Sharon patted Lea on the shoulder telling her to have a good day and leaned down to kiss Lea on the cheek. That was the last time Sharon ever saw Lea.

As we left the home, Sharon wanted me to take her to see Lea's house. She never quite believed me when I would describe the house, its condition, or the hoard to her. So, I told her I would take her. I didn't take her to say "See?" or" I told you so" – I took her because she asked me to.

Once in the house, I showed her what was once my bedroom. I showed her the folded-up cot that I slept on, the original holes in the walls that had been there since I was a little girl. The look on Sharon's face told me that she finally believed me. I *never* made any of this up. It gave me some validation knowing she finally understood how I actually grew up. After we left Lea's house, Sharon never said another word to me about it. I don't know if she felt guilty or angry. It was never my intent to make Sharon feel that way and I hoped she knew that.

After Sharon left to go back to Kahnawake, I finally started to see the end of the house nightmare. I knew the house and land would be sold at a later date to cover the expenses the state would incur for Lea's medical needs. My husband, son and I worked hard together clearing it out and, after almost five years, we finally got it done. We rented large dumpsters, threw away so much, some stuff I probably should have kept but had no place to put it. We rented a large storage unit for items I hoped to sell but even the storage unit became filled quickly. Unbeknownst to me, this would kickstart my ebay side hustle that I continued for many years.

2006

In Fall, 2006, I put the house and land on the market. At the time, the State had a huge lien on the property, and I knew I wasn't going to gain much monetarily from the sale. I knew the house would be torn down as it was uninhabitable. It didn't bother me. I was saying good-bye to something that did not hold good memories for me. I had several low-ball offers from independent buyers, and I knew the State would not approve the sale. Once I had a good offer, the State finally approved the sale in November, 2006, Lea started to decline faster. It was like she knew. Ironic.

Lea had been put in her own room on 24-hour bed care. She was unable to walk and could only manage to scream when she saw me or my husband. It was horrific at this point. She had contracted pneumonia and I was called for permission to put her in the hospital for treatment. I said I would be in to discuss the plan.

It had been a couple of months since my last visit. When my husband and I arrived, I could see Lea was lying on her side in the bed. She had lost most of her hair and looked almost skeletal. When she saw me, she would manage to scream but then be quiet. I asked her if she knew me and surprisingly, she would whisper 'Yes'. When I asked her what my name was, she became silent.

The nurse came in and we discussed the plan. Mike didn't like that we were discussing this in front of my mother as he believed Lea could absolutely comprehend all that we were discussing so we stepped into the hallway. I declined permission to have her go to the hospital for treatment at this point. What was the use? I could tell that her quality of life had diminished drastically. There was no need to have her suffer anymore. Physically, mentally, or emotionally. I decided then and there, as difficult as this would be, that I would stay by her side until she passed. She didn't have long.

I signed all the paperwork to begin administering comfort measures only. Lea's nurse started giving her morphine every few hours to help with whatever discomfort she was having, and the doses would be increased as time went on. I made arrangements to be out of work and they understood. I had just begun working at a new law firm and they were incredibly supportive. I went home to get a change of clothes and my iPod with some gentle ambient music to help comfort Lea during her transition. The entire staff came to say their good-byes when they learned she didn't have long. She would wake up from time to time and I would give her a gentle liquid mouth swab and talk to her. I would ask her from time to time again if she knew me and the answer would be "yes, I do" but she would never say my name or anything else.

As the next couple of days went on, the facility would let me rest in the bed next to hers although I didn't sleep. My husband would come by to drop off a change of clothes and sit with me for a while. I listened to her groaning and her breathing as it became more and more labored. I sat by her and talked to her about our life as mother and daughter. I told her I forgave her, and I hoped that she forgave me for not being the daughter she had hoped for but I prayed that she was proud of who I was at that moment as a woman, wife, mother and 'her' daughter. She never really responded to what I was saying. As she was still semi-conscious, I asked her in a whisper, holding her hand if she loved me and she whispered the words back "I guess." That was hard on my heart. My chest felt like a ton of bricks had been laid on it. I needed to push that down and not think about it as people were coming in and out. I was haunted by her words but also, I felt a warm peace blanket me because in my mind, that was a 'yes.' It was her way of saying she did love me.

Mike came in and sat with me as the end was nearing. He could see that I was in tears and I told him what she had just said a couple of hours before that. He hugged me. Martha, one of our dear friends, came in right after and offered prayers for Lea and for my peace. In that moment, as Lea's pain was ending, some of my own pain and hurt seemed to float away. I needed to forgive her.

Forgiveness has since become an integral part of my life for my own peace of mind. This is a prayer I find comforting:

The Forgiveness Prayer

"If I have harmed anyone in any way either knowingly or unknowingly through my own confusions, I ask their forgiveness. If anyone has harmed me in any way either knowingly or unknowingly through their own confusions, I forgive them. And if there is a situation, I am not yet ready to forgive, I forgive myself for that. For all the ways that I harm myself, negate, doubt, belittle myself, judge or be unkind to myself through my own confusions, I forgive myself."

Not too long after, when everyone left the room and I was alone with Lea, I watched her take her final breath as I held her hand. I was numb. It was surreal. I stayed with her body for a while just staring. Although I had suffered a tormented childhood of mental and physical abuse from Lea, I was relieved that she was no longer suffering her own pain. I felt dazed, not sure I had the strength to move but somehow forced myself. I reached out, took her hand, and kissed it gently. I then leaned in to kiss her forehead. Sadly, this was only one of a handful of times in my life that we ever shared a mother/daughter kiss.

I wobbly walked out to go out to the nurses' station to inform the nurse that Lea had just passed. Her nurse came in, pronounced Lea dead, and filled out the death certificate. She asked me if I was ok and I could only nod my head. The nurse called the funeral home. The funeral home was going to pick her body up the next morning and would call me to make final arrangements.

As I walked out of the nursing home to my car in a blur, I felt faint. I don't remember how I drove the two minutes home. I was in a complete fog.

At home, all I could do was just sit quietly in our spare bedroom alone for a while. Mike wanted me to lay down and rest, but my mind and my body wouldn't let me. My son had come home from school with tears in his eyes after his dad told him the news. While Ray was sad for me, at 13 years old, he never bonded with his grandmother and quite frankly, he barely remembered her. I kept him away from the 'Lea chaos!' That felt like a blessing in disguise.

I called Lea's brother, Paul, to let him know that his sister had passed. He was sad to hear about this. I told him that I was having a simple graveside service for her and that would be all. He accepted that. Or so I thought.

After that phone call, I felt like a wrecking ball had come down on top of me. I felt hard pain like I hadn't felt in years. As I sat, I stared blindly at the wall for a while. I couldn't think. My mind was stuck on the last images I had of Lea, dead.

It would be a couple of more hours before I emerged from the spare bedroom. I sat in the living room with Mike just talking about what I was going to do as far as planning my mother's graveside service. All of a sudden, the phone rang. I thought it was the funeral home calling with a time to meet the next day, but it wasn't. I could tell by the Caller ID that it was somebody I had long hoped to reconnect with. Funny how things happen on days like this. As I picked up the phone, my sadness turned to joy hearing the voice of my dear friend, Kim B. She lived with me in the last group home, and we had formed a very close bond while there, but hadn't seen or talked to each other in over 15 years.

"Hellooo?" I answered in my best pleasant voice I had for the moment.

"Is this Michelle?" She questioned.

"Is it really YOU?" I answered Kim, nearly in tears.

"Is it really YOU?" She answered back. Her voice was melodious to me at that moment.

"It's me...I'm so happy to hear your voice!" I cried.

"I'm so happy to hear yours too Michelle!" Kim answered with the same emotion.

"How are you? It's been years! Oh my gosh!" I needed to know how she was. I had missed her so much.

We talked about our lives and who we married. She knew I had gotten married and had a son. I knew she married her husband, John, after a long courtship. They didn't have children but had many fur babies. I had always hoped I would see her again and somehow, on this particular day, I knew we finally would. I felt Lea's spirit at work here. Lea liked to visit the girls at the group home when I was there. She particularly loved Kim and would bring her cigarettes every once in a while.

186

"Well wow! I think my mother's spirit is working here! You know she loved you, Kim!" I said.

"Oh no! When did she pass away?" She asked, not expecting the answer I was about to give her.

I looked at my watch, it had been almost 3 hours since Lea drew her last breath.

"Oh about 2:45 this afternoon," I answered quietly.

Dead silence. I didn't know if Kim was about to scream, cry or just hang up the phone. She was in shock.

"You mean TODAY?" Her voice was loud. She was in disbelief.

"Yea, today." I replied, taking a deep breath, trying so hard not to cry. "You know she loved you, Kim."

"Wow, Michelle! Yep, her spirit is definitely working! I have goosebumps! If I can do anything for you..." She was so tearful.

"Thank you! I'm just having a simple private graveside service for her." I explained.

"Thank God I'm sitting down!" She said, blown away by the news.

"Kim, my whole life has been rough with her, especially the last few years, I'm not going to lie." I told her.

"I know Michelle. I remember. I can't even imagine what you've gone through since our time together. But listen, after you get through the service, call me and we'll set that date to get together and talk about everything. We need that!" She was such a loving and genuine friend. She always was.

It was so good to hear Kim B.'s voice again and I think someone, or something, was telling us that we needed each other, now more than anything.

The next day, I went to the funeral home. I made the arrangements to have Lea cremated and I would pick up the urn when ready for the burial. They arranged for the cemetery to open the plot beside my father, Tom. There was no need for a Church service or funeral procession. I knew what Lea wanted ironically. Just a simple service.

On the day of Lea's burial, I had arranged for our friend Martha to perform the prayer service as she did for my mother-in-law, Barbara. It was something I think Lea would have liked. However, when we got to the cemetery, I was surprised to see quite a few people standing at the gravesite because I had planned for just a small private service. They were people I barely recognized, except for my Uncle Paul and someone that appeared to be a Catholic priest. My husband was about to let Uncle Paul know he crossed a line, but I asked him not to. I would handle this. As I walked up the path toward the open grave, holding my mother's urn, a cousin, Sandy, who I hadn't seen in many years came rushing up to me.

"Michelle!! It's your cousin Sandy! Oh, it's so good to see you! I'm so sorry about Aunt Lea," hugging me as I carried the urn. Oh, I remembered her. She was living with Rita at the same time as I was. She knew all about the 'adoption bombshell.'

"Hi Sandy, yes, I remember you." I was looking at the others who showed up as well, many other cousins I hadn't seen in years.

I wanted to scream: 'where the HELL have all of you been?! NOW you show up?!'

It was as if they crawled out from under a rock! But they were all so sorry for my loss. They all knew what happened to me. Not one of them showed any support to Lea or me over the years. Not one of them stepped up to see if I was ok behind closed doors with Lea or while I was in foster care. I was rather incensed, but I had to show dignity and bravery as we buried my mother. I was grateful that I had our friend, Martha, beside me for support.

It turned out that Uncle Paul had asked the Catholic priest to give a full mass at the gravesite without asking me. I wasn't having it. The priest stood there like he was about to take over and I stopped him asking Martha to perform the service as planned. I was clear in my decision. The priest respectfully stood back behind Uncle Paul and Martha began the service.

After Martha recited the prayers, I placed Lea's urn in the plot. Following my native custom, as a sign of respect, I wrapped her in a Mohawk made blanket. Lea's grave was then given a blessing. I felt the need to apologize to my cousins and Uncle Paul for not having a reception or lunch planned. I didn't expect anyone but Uncle Paul there. Nobody seemed surprised. It was as if they realized they might have overstepped just showing up.

As people disbursed, I watched my uncle give the Catholic priest some money apologizing to him for 'the misunderstanding. I followed my uncle to his car asking him to please wait a minute. He had no intention of speaking to me.

"I know you think I've done horrible things, but please let's clear the air, I loved my mother and I have never done anything wrong to her." I looked at him straight in the eyes.
"Oh ok." He nodded his head, closed his car door and drove off. That was the last time I saw him until his funeral about a year later.

After my mother's service, we stopped off at a restaurant with Martha and her husband for a quick bite as I had planned. Martha's husband had told me he overheard one of my cousins making plans to go back to my cousin Sandy's house for lunch, but they never mentioned it to me. I didn't think anything of it. It was just the way the family seemed to operate.

I will admit though that throughout the next year or so, my cousin Sandy did try to have me "rejoin" the family and have get-togethers at her house. It seemed as if the entire crew of cousins had drifted apart, and she wanted to get everyone together whenever we could. To be perfectly honest, I knew where her heart was, so I did attend some of these get-togethers. I wasn't comfortable and I think it showed. I actually held a holiday party at my home the following Christmas and invited the family, including Rita's daughter, Mary Ann and her family.

Basically, they came, ate, and left rather quickly. We didn't really talk about much of anything. My intentions were for all of us to gather and reflect on our parents who had now all passed. I was hoping for some bonding between us at least or some acceptance after all these years. Unfortunately, I wasn't feeling it. Eventually, we drifted apart again, and I no longer felt like I belonged with my adoptive family. Maybe it was just me.

Now that Lea was gone, I had to move on with my world but not without memories flooding back, boxes of stuff to go through and a lot of therapy through the years before and after the 'adoption bombshell' to even comprehend the word 'healing.'

I remember someone telling me something that always gives me a little bit of comfort, "You were the daughter she didn't deserve." I was.

Who Am I? I am the daughter Lea didn't deserve.

CHAPTER 13 – PASSPORT DEBACLE

2009-2011

When I turned 40, the news had reported that Canada was going to start requiring passports to enter the county. It used to be that Canada accepted your birth certificate and another form of ID (or sometimes just your word). Once Canada's requirement went into effect, I knew I was not going to be able to get into Canada or more importantly, get back into the United States without issue. I decided to apply for a US passport. Despite not having legal adoption papers, I wasn't concerned. I mean really, the 'official' birth/baptismal certificate from Kahnawake had said I was born in Connecticut. Nobody would deny that. Could they? Oh, but YES! They could and they did.

I applied for my US Passport. To my horror, I received a call regarding my birth and baptismal certificate, which was flagged as 'fraudulent.' WHAT?!!! I felt humiliated after being in America for 40 years, thinking I had dual citizenship as a Native American. Suddenly I was told I am not an American citizen and I had to take measures to amend my birth records. It didn't make sense because all of my schools, employers, the social security department, the department of motor vehicles and other agencies had accepted my birth/baptismal certificate without question. My father, Tom, 'took care' of all the paperwork thinking this gave me dual citizenship. Wrong. Interestingly, I had been given an American social security number as a baby. Times had changed.

This required me to go through two years of frustration with the American and Canadian governments proving that I was a Native American born in Canada. The paperwork alone was enough to make me vomit. I felt like all eyes were on me through radar. Here I was, at 40 years old, having lived in the United States my entire life, learning that I now needed to apply for a green card! WHAT?!

I was required to have my birth records amended before I could even apply for a green card under the Native American born in Canada category to be a permanent resident here in the United States. I wasn't even sure where to begin. My head hurt. I was incensed as I was forced to figure out where to start.

Before I applied for the green card, I figured I would try my hand at applying for a Canadian passport to maybe alleviate my situation and life could go on. So, I sent my application to the Canadian Passport Agency. I received a call from 'Otto,' an agent for the agency.

"Hello, is this Michelle Gauvreau?" Otto greeted me.
"Yes, it is." I replied.
"My name is Otto and I work for the Canadian Passport Agency," he introduced himself.
"I assume you're calling about my passport application?" I questioned.
"Yes, unfortunately we cannot approve your application. Your birth/baptismal certificate says you were born in Connecticut. You would have to apply for a U.S. Passport," he explained but I could tell that he was confused about my document. That damned certificate!
"I did apply for a U.S. Passport, Otto! I should explain my situation." I continued to explain my adoption, the fact that I was Native American from Kahnawake and how it was thought that I had dual citizenship.

"I'm so sorry you are going through this but unfortunately, we cannot approve your application at this time."

He sounded very sorry to tell me this. I felt like I had no country at this point. How do I prove myself? I had a lot to figure out.

I spoke with my birth mother, Sharon, that same day Otto called me, explained why I couldn't come up to visit then because of the requirements to have a passport. She was upset and didn't have any answers for me. I didn't expect her to. I just knew I would have to find a solution, no matter what it took.

The next day, I received a call back from Otto at the Canadian Passport Agency that I didn't expect.

"Hi Michelle. I have some information I think you might find helpful." he seemed happy to tell me whatever it was.

"Oh, well I hope it's good information," I was very leery.

"I think it might be. I spoke to my director about your situation, and she indicated that you might want to get your newborn medical records from the hospital you were born at, get your birth mother's as well and send a letter to Etat Civil (Vital Records Office) in Quebec explaining your situation and ask that they amend your birth certificate. Etat Civil is not easy to contend with regarding these types of situations and I'm not going to guarantee that they will agree to amend your birth certificate, but it's worth trying especially in your situation." Otto was a huge help to me.

"Otto, you really made my day. Thank you for talking to your director about my situation." I was practically in tears.

"Michelle, you have a very unique case. We'll do all we can to help. If you are able to get your birth records amended, we'll approve your passport application." He told me.

"I'm totally on it!" I said as we hung up.

In the meantime, I had made an appointment to see an immigration attorney. I explained my situation and he agreed the wise thing for me to do was to get my birth record amended, get my Canadian passport and then I can move forward with my green card application and that he would help me with the process to the tune of several thousand dollars that I surely didn't have then. I thanked him for our initial consultation, but I was determined to figure this out on my own.

I spoke to Sharon again and asked her if she would sign a medical authorization from the hospital that would give me permission to get her medical records regarding my birth and I explained that I would get my own records there as well for the purpose of getting my birth records amended with Etat Civil. I also explained that I would need an affidavit explaining the circumstances of my birth. I offered to draft it and would email it to one of Sharon's sisters to print out and bring it to her to sign. Sharon was more than willing to sign whatever she had to for me to visit. I was blessed that she did this for me.

As I waited for her to mail me the document I needed, I started to draft my letter to Etat Civil explaining my unusual circumstances asking that they amend my birth records but not change my parents' names on the certificate so as to not cause more scrutiny. It would not have been a big deal except for the fact that I knew my birth father would never sign off on his name being put on the amended document. So, I left my adoptive parents' names, Lea and Tom on the document. Sharon and I were ok with that. Once I received the documents from Sharon, I faxed a letter to the hospital requesting our medical records which I received within a week. So far, things were moving in the right direction. I sent off the letter I had drafted along with Sharon's Affidavit and our medical records to Etat Civil in Quebec. I anxiously waited two weeks before I decided to call them to see if they had in fact received the documents.

When I called Etat Civil, I expected to be denied any amendment of my birth certificate. However, I was pleasantly surprised when I was told that given my circumstances, they were going to approve the amendment. I cried and nearly fell to the floor. I thanked them from the bottom of my heart. I was told my case was very unusual and they were sorry it did not raise a flag in the 1990s when all vital records were transferred from the reservation Churches to the Canadian government. I was honest and explained that I never expected to have an issue such as this. I was understood. Finally.

Within two or so weeks, I had my newly Amended Birth Certificate(s) in my hand. I promptly sent this to Otto at the Canadian Passport Agency. Within a few more weeks, I held my Canadian passport in my hands. I almost wanted to glue it to my hand. Almost.

Even though I finally had my Canadian passport, I still would not be able to travel until I had my US Permanent Resident card in hand. I had heard and read stories about others having a hard time getting back into the United States from Canada. I did not want to be another one of those stories. I refused.

After much thought and debate, I eventually wrote a hefty $900 check and applied for my US Permanent Resident Card. I was incensed at the idea. Me? A Native American woman born in Canada having to get a US Permanent Resident Card? I was told by the immigration attorney that I initially consulted with that I should get the card and then after 5 years, I should apply to become a US citizen. Seriously? I was furious. I felt like I was having an out of body experience when he told me that. I felt like I should have been protected by some sort of rule of Native American Sovereignty.

Within about six weeks after my initial application, I received an appointment letter to come into the Homeland Security / Immigration Department to discuss my application. As I arrived for my appointment, I was required to bring all my identification, my new passport, and my birth certificate. I brought an entire folder of all that I thought they would need. I was drilled with questions by the agent handling my application.

"Why didn't you apply for a Permanent Resident Card when you married your husband?" She was very stern pointing her bony finger at me. Oh no, they weren't putting that on me.

"I have lived here since I was a newborn. I am Native American and was under the belief that I had dual citizenship. That was until I applied for a US Passport." I explained.

"What made you think you had dual citizenship?" She looked at me like I was from outer space.

"I just told you, I'm Native American, born in Canada" I replied firmly.

"You still should have applied through your husband!" Again, pointing a finger at me. The hairs on my neck stood up!

"No. I'm going to do this the right way. I've been here since I was a newborn in 1969. I didn't know I was going to have to go through hell and back now. Schools, agencies, social security and the DMV all accepted my initial birth certificate! This only happened because I applied for a US Passport," I explained hotly. If I was going to get a US Permanent Resident card, it was going to be under the S13 category as a Native American born in Canada.

"I'll have to review your application more. Do you have your blood quantum letter proving your 50% blood lineage?" She asked, not thinking I would actually know what she was talking about. Joke was on her. I pulled out the certified letter from Kahnawake stating my blood quantum and lineage. I was ready and organized. The agent did not know what to say. At the end of the appointment, she said she would re-evaluate my application and I would receive another appointment letter.

A few weeks later, I received another letter from Immigration. It wasn't another appointment letter. It was a letter demanding further paperwork or proof of my Native American lineage. They wanted me to obtain my maternal *and* paternal grandparents' long form birth certificates so that my blood quantum could be proved. My own paperwork wasn't enough, I guess. As I researched how to obtain my grandparents' birth certificates, I learned it would cost me nearly $800.00. I was NOT spending another dime to get these birth certificates and decided to pay a visit to the Immigration Department myself. I made an online 'urgent' appointment for the next day.

As I arrived at Immigration, I went through the Homeland Security routine of being patted down, going through the x-ray machine, and having my purse dumped out and inspected. I had to take a number and wait for the next agent. It would be a good hour or more, so I sat in deep thought about all that I had gone through in the last year and a half with getting my Canadian passport and now going through the process of obtaining my permanent residency. It had been a lot to comprehend. Finally, my number was called.

"Hi Michelle, how can I help you today?" As I approached the agent's window, I recognized the young lady who was assisting the agent on my previous visit.

"Hi there. I have an issue with this recent letter from the previous agent requiring that I get my paternal/maternal grandparents' birth certificates proving my Native American lineage. I've shown my own paperwork proving who I am. I'm not prepared to spend another $800 to get paperwork that really won't prove anything more than I have." I explained.

"Hmm. You know my mother-in-law, also Native American from Canada, just went through the same thing and I was able to help her bypass having to get more paperwork." She explained.

"Really? Is there any way I can avoid this as well and not waste my time or money?" I asked. I was stressed. I would have dropped to my knees and begged but I think she already knew I was desperate at this point.

"Let me go talk to my supervisor. Go have a seat for now." She smiled at me and walked to the back of their cubicles where her supervisor was sitting.

In what seemed like forever, I sat there nervous. I reorganized my paperwork binder at least three times. Finally, I heard her calling my name. I shook as I walked up to the service window. Naturally I was expecting the worst answer.

"Michelle, you should have your green card in about two weeks." She told me happily.

Wait, WHAT?!...Am I in a dream? Did I just hear her say two weeks?

"Oh my God! Really? There's nothing else you need me to do?" I felt dazed.

"No, you're all set. My supervisor felt you did enough to prove yourself," she explained.

"Well, I don't believe I can ever thank you but THANK YOU!" I wanted to hug her.

I hurried out of there before they could change their minds. I rushed home. It was cause to celebrate!

As promised within two weeks, I finally received my US Permanent Resident Card. Another huge weight was lifted off and I was free to travel with my Canadian passport and U.S. permanent resident card. Freedom had rung!

Emotionally, I was able let go of the two years of struggling to prove who I was legally. It wouldn't serve me to stay angry about the situation. It was a huge learning process that I do not take for granted. I would tell anyone going through the same to stay the course and eventually you'll get there.

Who Am I? I am a woman, free to wander the world.

CHAPTER 14 - SPECIAL REPORT

While going through the passport debacle, I came across a report that was filed by the Department of Children and Youth Services (now known as the Department of Children and Families) filed on September 11, 1986. This report was filed as a result of me being taken out of Lea's home and placed in a Salvation Army Shelter before officially entering the foster care system. Reading certain paragraphs of this report today still causes sleepless nights and waves of anxiety as it was based *solely* on the statement that Lea provided at the time. Did she really hate me that much? What do you think?

DEPARTMENT OF CHILDREN AND YOUTH SERVICES REPORT FILED IN 1986

STUDY FOR SUPERIOR COURT – JUVENILE MATTERS ON PETITION REGARDING UNCARED-FOR CHILD

Lea told a state worker that she was not involved when Michelle's custody arrangements were made after she was born and she believed at the time that Michelle's "adoption" was legal. When she found out about it later, she was afraid she would lose Michelle if she tried to change the situation.

My Thoughts:

In reality, after I was told about my "adoption," Lea said that all my adoption paperwork was in Canada. I suspect she knew that my "adoption" was illegal and that there was no paperwork. Further, she never had the finances to take care of the situation as it meant contacting Tom's family to get in touch with Sharon. See Chapter 1.

The birth mother, Sharon, has not responded to the Department of Children and Youth Services regarding the uncared-for-petition. However, she wrote a letter to the court leaving the decision up to Michelle as to where she would like to live.

According to Lea and Michelle, Sharon was believed to an alcoholic and in poor health and it does not appear that she is able to provide an appropriate home for Michelle. In addition, Michelle has not expressed a wish to live with her natural mother in Canada.

My thoughts:

Sharon did, in fact, invite me to come back to live with her and my birth family. She left the decision up to me but keep in mind, I was just 16 years old. A confused kid. After I came back from Canada, I believe I had a bit of culture shock and at the time it was a foreign lifestyle I didn't know if I could handle. Remember, I was only 16. It was not an easy decision, but I felt staying in Connecticut, despite my circumstances, was the right decision for me at the time. See Chapter 4.

Michelle was picked up by Tom when she was a few days old and brought to Connecticut. Tom and Lea had been married since 1958 and had no children of their own. Tom died in July, 1972.

According to Lea, Michelle was a healthy child and her growth and development was normal. She started kindergarten at a local public school and attended grades one through six at a Catholic School. She repeated second grade but had no other problems until she started Middle School at age twelve. Lea reported that, at the time, she started lying and stealing at home and in the community. She also refused to take a shower or bath and was made fun of by her peers because of her body odor. Lea took Michelle to the Community Child Guidance Clinic for therapy and also received counselling from the school social worker.

My thoughts:

It should be noted that we rarely had running water making it difficult to bathe. Laundry was done once a month at the local laundry mat. I was bullied and harassed by my peers for more than that. As for the statement Lea made about my lying and stealing, I can say unequivocally, that was not true in any sense, and I chalk it up to her mental illness. See Chapter 4.

In the summer of 1985, Michelle was told by Lea's sister-in-law that she was adopted and that her natural mother had a large extended family living in Canada. Lea had planned to tell Michelle that she was not her biological mother when she reached her 18th birthday.

My thoughts:

I honestly do not believe that Lea ever planned on telling me. I do believe that if I had not gone into foster care, she would have thrown me out on my 18th birthday. See Chapter 5.

Michelle was able to track down her grandmother, Sharon's mother, on the Caughnawaga Indian Reservation and she contacted her by telephone. Subsequently, she spent the summer on the Reservation where she met her biological mother, maternal grand-mother and her half-brother.

When she returned to Lea at the end of the summer, Lea told her that she would longer provide a home for her because she was never legally adopted and, therefore, not Lea's responsibility.

My thoughts:

I was happy that I found Sharon and my birth family. I was grateful for the opportunity to meet them. When I returned home to Lea in September 1985, I was floored at the way Lea treated me. I believe she was unable to handle the truth and our reality. Mental illness doesn't go away. See Chapter 7.

On August 30, 1985, the Department of Children and Youth Services received the first referral from the Community Child Guidance Clinic requesting placement of Michelle due to Lea's unwillingness to provide a home for her.

My thoughts:

For the record, I had no idea that Lea was in the process of kicking me out of the house. See Chapter 7 for the full story.

On November 8, 1985, the Police Department was involved because of a physical confrontation between Lea and Michelle where Lea struck Michelle in the face and threatened to kill her if she was not removed from her home. Consequently, Michelle was placed in the Salvation Army Shelter in Hartford and, when Lea still refused to take her home, she was placed in a foster home.

My thoughts:

Lea never disclosed the full truth to the police or the social worker. She did more than strike me in the face. On that night, Lea had started a fight with me. While I don't remember what was said, I do remember her screaming at me and chasing me with a leather strap, striking me wherever she could as well as punching me, causing multiple bruises and a bloody nose. When the police officer arrived, she did threaten to kill me. See Chapter 7 for the full story.

Michelle is without a legal guardian in the United States. Her natural mother has stated in a letter that Michelle could come live with her but is leaving the decision up to Michelle. Michelle has told this state worker that she does not want to live on the Reservation. However, since her mother has invited her to live with her, apparently for the first time, Michelle vacillates a great deal in her feelings as to where she wants to live.

My thoughts:

While it is true that Sharon did invite me to come live in Kahnawake at the time, I truly did not know whether I wanted to live there. It was a different world to me, one that I didn't think I would be able to handle well. See Chapter 4.

This worker contacted the Bureau of Indian Affairs before uncared-for-petitions were filed and was told that the Mohawks of Caughnawaga Reservation are not a federally recognized tribe in the United States and that, therefore, the Indian Child Welfare Act, in which the tribe has to be notified whenever a change of guardianship or an adoption involving an Indian child takes place, does not apply to Michelle.

My thoughts:

I remember distinctly being told at the time that since I was Native American born in Canada, that I had dual citizenship and should have no worries. I remember thinking that the State should have sought to correct my citizenship at the time I was in placement but it was never acted on. See Chapter 12 for full story about my Passport Debacle.

As of this report, 1986, Michelle has no home in Connecticut and no legal guardian. She is in need of therapy to help her work through her feelings of rejection, first by her natural family and then by her psychological mother as well.

She is currently in placement, a group home which will provide structure, supervision and guidance. She will also be provided with therapy from a local community agency and she will be able to complete her education. It appears that this plan meets her needs and is in her best interest.

Therefore, it is recommended that Michelle be committed to the Commission of the Department of the Children and Youth Services in order to continue her placement at the group home and to provide her with a legal guardian.

CHAPTER 15 – HEALING BEGINS

I believe it probably was my stubborn Native strength, my perseverance, and the therapy I received as an adult that got me through almost everything. I'm not saying I'm happy every minute. I'm not always grounded either. Who is? I just choose to be satisfied. Whatever is challenging, I try to just push myself through. Deep breathing also helps me to cope. To destress, I close my eyes, take deep breaths, and breathe out at least three times. Three slow inhales through my nose and three slow exhales through my mouth. It immediately helps.

I have learned over the years to reframe my story. I have finally accepted my past with a different perspective. I'm now able to appreciate all that I have.

Am I still angry with my adoptive mother, Lea? Not anymore. I realize now that she was mentally ill. I didn't know that as a child. It wasn't something society acknowledged during that era. I know she suffered, and I had suffered with her but, I have since found a level of peace allowing me to release any lingering anger. Despite having forgiven her, I still sometimes struggle with waves of emotion from my past. Perhaps when she put me into the foster care system as a teenager, unknowingly, she was trying to save us both.

I was angry that Lea intentionally cut Tom's family out of my life. My adoptive father was a good man. I know my life would have been blessed had he lived, and how I wish I could have been a part of his extended family growing up. It was not to be at the time. I think Lea feared she would lose me. Years later, just before she died, I found several cards and letters from Tom's family that Lea hid from me. I knew there were secrets, many that did not reveal themselves until I was an adult. For instance, she never told me at the time that Tom had been married before with a son, my brother, David or that I had a sister from another relationship Tom had in Maryland. I was also shocked to learn that Lea had also been previously married once before to a man who lived in Harlem, New York. It seemed that these little surprises kept rolling in over the years.

Obviously, the biggest secret that Lea had kept from me was that I was adopted. *Illegally* adopted. By the time I found out, there was already an empty void in my life. I never felt true love in my own home. I felt like an outcast in school and with Lea's extended family. This is why I was determined to find my birth mother. I knew Lea would never take me back to Kahnawake herself which is why I jumped on a bus at 15 years old in search of answers.

Am I angry with my birth mother? No. Sharon didn't give me up willingly. I understand now that she gave me up out of love knowing my grandmother was probably right. My grandmother knew Sharon was incapable of raising me at the time, so they did what they thought was best for me. I never felt abandoned by them. Their door was always open for me in anticipation of the day I would want to seek them out and is still wide open today. For that, I'll forever be grateful.

I was fortunate that the right man came along to adopt me even if the adoption was a farce. What was unfortunate was that same man, my father, Tom, died when I was so young. It was he who would teach me the traditions of the Mohawk community. He had plans to teach me Mohawk, French and German languages. Ohhh, the list of goals went on, but he was unable. That's ok. I know at least he loved me.

Reflecting on my past is sometimes hard for me and for others to understand. Many get very confused by my story. Before and after Lea passed away, I found myself struggling with depression and insomnia. I saw several therapists and a psychiatrist over the years, many of whom would eventually put me on several medications that didn't seem to work. While medications are helpful and necessary for many who struggle, I felt I needed to feel a more natural state and wanted a more holistic approach to finding my peace. However, through it all, I managed to live through my darkest days, months, and years. After Lea died, I knew I needed to find my purpose. Surely there must be a more productive path in my life's journey.

My saving grace through much of this as an adult was my holistic therapist, Dee. I was in my 30s, stressed at work, going through the roller coaster of emotions with Lea being in the nursing homes, cleaning out the house, and eventually having to deal with her death all while taking care of my own family. It took its toll. I felt so sick. My entire life felt like a whirlwind of emotions. I did not want medication. I finally felt at ease as I started my holistic therapy. As I explained the stories of my life, Dee was incredibly supportive and taught me to deeply breathe through my stress. I learned to use imagery throughout my sessions. Luckily Dee was knowledgeable about the native culture and its belief that we are all connected to a spirit animal. The assumption is that all animals bring messages that guide us through life. I found comfort in that. I was able to find my inner child and discovered my spirit animal was the Bear, being that I was born into the bear clan amongst my native family. I've learned that my connection to the Bear taught me without a doubt to set boundaries and not compromise when pressured. Like the Bear, I also realized that I would 'hibernate' during various times of my life by keeping to myself and disconnecting from certain friendships and family members. I now feel I need to soften the Bear claw at times.

In my native culture, we believe that our Creator assigned animals to show himself through them together with the sun, the moon, and the stars, they work together to guide mankind. Those spirits in animal form are called animal guides, which are believed to teach us, empower us, and heal us. In some indigenous cultures, they are called totem animals.

Today, when I see certain animals, whether in real life or in my dreams, I breathe in and try to find their message to me. I think about the first person who comes to mind and try to absorb any vibrations from the energy exuded.

If you are Native American and/or a member of the First Nations, an animal clan is with you for life, ones that are supposed to guide you through tough times and make sure your path is smooth. Each clan has its personality. For me, I was born into the Bear clan (you are accepted into the clan that your mother is a part of). The Bear is telling me to be courageous and appreciate life. Bear is up for the task and stands for protection, the value of rest and privacy, particularly in a busy society. There seems to be many variations of the personalities and beliefs within each of the clans but in the end, to me, seem to equal the same value. Community.

While I believe in the values of the clans in my community, I also believe in the lessons of other animals and their messages if one should appear before messages. These were teachings that I learned from other nations as well, through powwows and other reservations that I visited over time. Keep in mind, these lessons can apply to everyone in the world, not just Native Americans.

Birds seem to always have messages for me, and most of them are good. One example would be the falcon that appeared before me on my balcony outside my office window on the 28th floor. Wow! It was beautiful. I had to take a moment to look at it. I suddenly felt empowered. I searched my books and medicine cards on animals to find that the falcon was telling me to keep going., Fly high. I believe it was validation to continue writing this book of my own truth, raw and vulnerable. This was very powerful for me.

This has sparked a new mission of teaching others the importance of human connection to animals and how we can learn from them. More on this in my forthcoming book.

Through my holistic therapy, Dee connected me with a massage therapist, Marni. We vibed immediately. She was mystically beautiful. Her touch was cathartic. I felt the release of the pain I wasn't aware I'd held within my body since I was a child. Sometimes I would burst into tears as soon as she touched me. I needed to release myself from the emotion and physical pain I had buried for so many years.

Over the next couple of years, I had regular massage therapy and lots of holistic therapy. At the time, I paid out of pocket for the private treatment with Dee and Marni to feel better about myself. It allowed me to see the light through the darkness. While massage therapy / holistic treatment can be expensive, many health insurance companies are now seeing its value and may cover some of the costs. I was able to come out of a fog that clouded much of my life. It was a necessity to invest in myself for my overall health. I was finally able to give myself love.

Today, while I am not in therapy now, I hold on to the support that was given to me by Dee and Marni. They will always remain an integral part of my life. Although Marni has since passed, occasionally, I still treat myself to a massage when my life gets a little overwhelming, but it will never be the same. For Dee, I hold tight to all that she taught me about breathing and imagery. This is what gets me through the dark days and good days too.

In 2010, I reconnected with several of the girls I lived with in foster care now more than 20 years earlier at the time. I put the reunion together myself. It was challenging to locate everyone, but social media helped. After connecting with many from these group homes, it was heart-warming to find that we all survived and most of us were doing well. We seemed to bond again quickly, just like when we were teenagers. That will forever stay with me. Some of the girls had moved out of state and some were still in Connecticut. I still get together with those who live locally on occasion, we just hang out and chat about the foster homes, group homes and life today. Some of us are married with children, others stayed single. It almost seems impossible that a few are now actually grandmothers. Having this friendship bond has been yet another saving grace for me. Human connection is invaluable.

Sadly a few years later, we lost one of the girls from our group home whom so of us many were close to. Kim B. died of breast cancer at just 41 years old in 2013. Her death broke our hearts, especially mine. She and I were extremely close during our group home years and had rekindled our bond as adults since the day Lea died.

My life has had so many experiences, good and bad. Sprinkled with many confusing times, perhaps more than the average person. I feel fortunate that I was able to meet my birth mother's side of the family and they had accepted me with open arms. To this day, I feel welcome in Kahnawake. The Mohawk community has proven to be nothing more than a pillar of grace when it comes to family. I am so proud of my bloodline.

It hurts my heart that I am not in touch with my birth family in Canada as much as I should be. I check in on my mother through other nearby family members to make she is ok as she prefers a more private life at this time. I miss my mother and my brother.

A Life Of Searching For Love and Acceptance Everywhere

Through many years of therapy, I have come to learn that throughout my life, I had been trying to fill a void in my heart. A void created from a lack of true unconditional love throughout my childhood. When I was young, I trusted a lot of the wrong people. Some might have thought, "what was she thinking?" I was desperate, I guess. Desperate for love and attachment to someone or something. Some people, older men in particular, took advantage of me in such a vulnerable state. I didn't understand the concept of self-respect. Growing up in a household sans love, how would I have learned about love and respect? I've since realized that my lifestyle at the time was a common trait among young girls who were lonely and lost.

I would hang on to people who showed me the slightest interest or attention. In the end, I was hurt and disappointed many times until I started looking out for myself, realizing I should never depend on people who say they will but don't. It took a while to learn that but eventually, it happened, and my thick skin came in. I don't get as emotional as I once did over things. Now I just let it roll and take each day as it comes. I choose to smile and help others going through similar situations. The good that has emerged is my passion to help others. My mission now is helping adoptees navigate their own challenges. We can all choose to be okay each day. I know I am not alone, and neither are you. I am here with you.

Over the years, I would learn hard lessons and start becoming a better judge of character. I learned who to stay away from and who to keep in my life. I consider everything a blessing or a lesson. I like to focus on the good in relationships and relish the memories rather than dwell on what happened to make that relationship fail. I don't regret the failed relationships in my life, past or present. There are some relationships I would still like to fix.

I lost out on relationships that could have been positive if Lea had not cut off so much of the social world to me. I missed out on so many friends, opportunities, and family connections in my life because of her. Since I was not given that privilege, I had to eventually forge my own path without any guidance.

Honestly, I'm not angry or sad anymore about my adoption today. I look at this as a trail that I am still walking.

I am, however, mindful that everyone's adoption is unique. There are circumstances all around the world even crazier than mine, especially in the Native American communities. I take everything one day at a time. Am I grateful for the journey? Every day. Some days things hit me hard, but I come out of it and go on about my business. I'm finally content.

Am I sorry for my childhood anger towards my Aunt Rita for telling me about my adoption? One hundred percent. In retrospect, she provided the entry to my undiscovered heritage. Had she not told me, I'm not sure I would have ever known.

Today, I think adoption is a wonderful thing as long as it is done legally, and the child or children are raised knowing their background and culture. I know there are circumstances where there is no other choice but adoption or foster care and sometimes causing confusion about their background. I know that there are many cases where the child will never know their ancestral roots or culture. I completely understand that. I have absolute compassion about adoption and foster care but there is so much room for improvement. My own adoption drama may seem like it was ripped from a Lifetime movie, but it was a story that needed to be told, nonetheless.

If nothing else, my journey through the fog gave me newfound clarity of purpose. I realize I can no longer dwell on the what ifs.

I believe my crazy 'adoption' made me a more compassionate person as an adult, having been through physical and mental abuse, foster homes, group homes and so much more. The path I chose was to simply be a good person. My story needed to be told.

The energy we put out into the universe is what we will get back. I choose positivity. Anyone else's opinions of me or what I 'should' do doesn't matter anymore. I survived and gained much wisdom in my fifty-plus years on this earth and it's not over yet. We all should continue chasing our dreams!

Do I go back and think about things or certain events? Absolutely. Do I still get sad or angry? Absolutely! I wish things could have been different. My reality cannot be changed. The only thing I can do is share my experiences and hopefully help the next adoptee realize that it is okay to struggle emotionally at times and still come out 'okay' on the other side. I have grown stronger and no longer ask myself, "why me?". I am not a victim.

I had an epiphany one day and it all makes sense to me now. I do believe that there was a plan for me, and I felt that I didn't truly belong with either my adoptive family or my birth family but the plan was for me to make my own family and I did. I married a good man and made a family with him. Through the years of bonding, growing, good times, bad times, I find that I am in a good place today. I have been able to look at things with more of an open mind, but I'll never say it was easy. I've had my moments where depression creeps in, but I pull myself back up and into the light.

I think every adoptee needs to eventually process their emotions to be able to say, "I'm okay now" or "I'm not okay." Everyone has their own story to tell. I think recognizing one's feelings must be expressed in order to heal. With time comes perspective. There are no expiration dates on feelings. Feelings will come and go like clouds on a windy day. Conscious breathing is my anchor.

My one hope for all adoptees is that they know they are 'enough' and that they matter in this world, no matter the story they carry with them, good or bad. You can turn any wound into wisdom. My upbringing may not have been great, but I have found a meaningful life now. I still strive for a peaceful life in the world, not just for me, but for all of us.

On a visit to Kahnawake just before the COVID pandemic hit, as the night fell, I stood on the St. Lawrence seaway, watching a ship sail by and seeing the dancing lights of the south side of Montreal. It all seemed a world away from the native village I was born in, on September 2, 1969. In my mind I hear the powwow drum and singers in the wind, and I see native dancers dancing in their regalia around the circle of fire showing their resilience and strength around me in a world that I was supposed to be a part of. That's where my strength and purpose must come from. Fate had a plan for me, just as it does for you.

So, who am I? So many events in my life shaped me into who I am today and that will never change. Growing up between two countries and two cultures, I now tell myself:

"I am strong, I am thankful, I stand
as a proud Mohawk woman. I am Michelle."

213

NOTE OF INTEREST …

I often think of other Native American babies who had been adopted illegally like me. Statistics show that over 50% of native babies and children are either in foster care or adopted. I still wonder how this can be, but I know that answers are not easy because so much was undocumented.

I was shocked to learn that back in the 1960s (some reports indicate even from the turn of the 20th century) many babies and children who were not adopted into families were sent to Catholic residential schools throughout North America. This has been referred to as 'child-scooping.' Some children were even taken from their homes under the guise of a proper education. It turned out to be propaganda with racism and genocide in its ugliest form to wipe out the Native American race. An ethnic cleansing behind closed doors via corporal punishment with abuse, starvation, and murder at the hands of cruel nuns or priests and were buried in unmarked graveyards. In 2021 with the aid of sonar/ultrasound machines hundreds of children's remains were found in the ruins of one Canadian residential school in British Columbia. This made news around the world. Since then, thousands more were found buried in other closed down residential schools across Canada. TV journalist, Anderson Cooper, did a segment that showed survivors sharing their horrific stories of the abuse they had suffered. I shudder at the thought that I may not have survived if I had been placed at one of these residential schools.

The Vatican initially resisted many calls to address the horrific acts by the Catholic residential schools against Indigenous children. However, July 25, 2022, Pope Francis travelled to Canada offering his prayers, condolences, and apologies to all Indigenous nations on behalf of the Catholic Church for what was done to their children for so many years. It was very emotional to watch.

It is possible I might also have been sent to one of these residential schools. These Indigenous children lost their children, families, heritage and more importantly their community. I felt the same but was lucky to get back a bit of my heritage and culture thanks to my birth family on the reservation and my Connecticut foster parents who exposed me to native traditions through. I will never get everything back, but I am happy with what I have now.

About The Author

Michelle Rice-Gauvreau is a native Mohawk woman born in Canada and raised in Connecticut via an illegal adoption, which was commonplace for many native babies throughout many years across North America. She is a compassionate advocate for all adoptees looking for their own truth, peace and hope. She hopes to instill her strength to any adoptee struggling to find their way.

Michelle now works as a legal professional for a prestigious law firm. She resides in Connecticut with her husband of many years, her adult son, and her two senior cats. She enjoys traveling and learning more about native cultures far and wide.

Contact Michelle

Michelle is available for interviews and/or speaking engagements in person or virtually.

This book, *Who Am I?* is available to purchase in bulk at a discounted rate.

For more information or to connect with Michelle directly:

Email: info@michellegauvreau.com

Website: www.michellegauvreau.com

Facebook Page: @IAmAnAdoptee

Michelle will try to personally respond to each and every inquiry.

RECOMMENDED RESOURCES

There is a continuing problem with adoption throughout the globe. I want to raise awareness for adoptees and adoptive parents as well. While, of course, there are countless adoptive parents who are providing loving homes for many children, unfortunately, there are still many children, especially from indigenous communities who are illegally adopted, exploited, trafficked or murdered at a relentless rate.

Books

The Girl In The Photograph – Senator Byron L. Dorgar
Adoption's Hidden History: From Native American Tribes to Locked Lives – Mary S. Payne
Through Adopted Eyes - A Collection of Memoirs from Adoptees – Elena S. Hall
You Don't Look Adopted – Anne Heffron
You Don't Know How Lucky You Are: An Adoptee's Journey Through the American Adoption Experience – Rudy Owens

Facebook Pages

I Am An Adoptee – *this is my personal page to support all adoptees looking for help, inspiration, love, and peace to get them through the day.*
Adoptees Connect, Inc.
The Evolving Adoptee
This Adoptee Life
The Chameleon

Websites

For murdered or missing indigenous women:
nativehope.org/missing-and-murdered-indigenous-women-mmiw

For American Indian/First Nations Adoptees:
blog.americanindianadoptees.com

For Canadian Adoption Records by Proving
originscanada.org/adoption-records/by-province

Author's Website, Blog and Store
www.michellegauvreau.com

Podcasts
thearchibaldproject.com
adoptionnowpodcast.com

MY LOVE LETTER TO THE GOOD ONES

Dear Adoptive Parents,

My heart is full of joy for moms and dads who have adopted children. It is truly the greatest gift you can give a child, who in turn, becomes the greatest gift to a parent. These children have a safe place in your hearts, lives and homes.

Adoption is beautiful. There are so many children in need around the world. I admire adoptive parents for showing up, for being united in the care of and devotion to raising your children. You are a coveted and amazing community. The court systems should take note of how well you care for and love these children. In the meantime, *I thank you*!

Unfortunately, there are some adopted children who still may struggle with their identity and may want to one day search for their biological parents for information. Some searches may end up in disappointment while others may have a happy ending. I ask that you to always be honest with your children. I wasn't so lucky. Sadly, it's a growing problem globally.

If your children are of a different race, ethnicity and/or from another country, please instill and celebrate their culture and traditions with them. That will be very important as they become adults. If you know your child's history or the birth family, please keep that information on hand along with any original adoption documentation. Please keep a journal of your family's history for them. Trust me, your children will want to read it someday.

Continue being kind, continue being open, continue being honest and please *always*, love them.

With love and fondness,

Michelle

This letter extends to my own foster parents, Geoff and Elaine. You were wonderful foster parents. You stood by me and many other foster children over the years. As a teenager, I know you dealt with both good and bad times with me, but you gave me a glimpse into my native culture and for that I will forever be grateful. At such a pivotal time in my life you gifted me the missing puzzle piece in my own search for my identity. I love you both more than you will ever know. ~Michelle

LOVE LETTER TO MY BIRTH MOTHER, SHARON

Dear Sharon,

I like to think that you are finding a new understanding while reading this book, because in my mind, *you* were here with me through every page written. I hope you now feel some sense of pride for me, your daughter. I have nothing but love and pride to give back to you.

Your sacrifice to give me up was one of the hardest things you ever had to do. While you didn't want to give me up, you never gave up on me. Still today, I feel that. I can't imagine how you felt for 15 years before we met in 1984. You told me you would drive around, find a quiet place and cry. I cried along with you after I was told I was adopted. I felt a sense of loss in everything I knew at a very dark time. If I didn't fight to meet you as a teen, I doubt I ever would have been allowed.

When we finally met, I remember staring at you in wonder. How beautiful you were and still are. You hugged me so tight. I was happy that I had come to visit that summer so that we could get to know each other. You kept looking at me as though it was a dream that I was standing in front of you. I felt the same. But more than that, I felt that instant connection. I believe we shared a moment of mother-daughter love, something I had never felt before.

Over the many years we have known each other, I have watched you. I want to think that you passed your strength on to me. I've learned that we have to get through hardships and make choices that carve our lives. Just as these choices and hardships can become songs or disappointments, I had a choice to portray myself as a victim of circumstance or as a proud Mohawk woman walking with valor and grace. I chose valor and grace. Despite it all, I have peace.

I've learned that the secret to adoption is that no matter the circumstance or the pain of separation, every story begins with a mother's love and ultimate sacrifice. Sacrifices have the power to remind others that they are worthy of a life that should be good and lived fully. You gave me the gift of life. Thank you.

Love, ♥ Your daughter

Photo Reflections

My Adoptive Parents

Tom

Lea

Us

Tom

Tom, Mohawk Ironworker, on the Twin Towers 1960s/1970s

Tom, 1940s

Tom dancing in his native regalia

Tom in deep thought

Lea

Lea with her brothers, Joseph (left) and Paul (right), late 1920s

Lea, 21

Lea intently watching something.

Lea, 81

Tom & Lea

Tom and Lea at a wedding, 1970

Tom and Lea, 1950s

My Birth Family

Sharon

Eddie

Sharon

Me, Sharon and my brother, Mike, 1986

My Aunt Sue(L) with Sharon(R) 1980

My maternal Grandmother, Mary, 1987

My brother Mike, age 17

Eddie

The moment we met,
November, 1999

Eddie's daughter Tina and I
meeting for the first time.

Tina, Eddie and I
1999

Saying Goodbye

Sharon, Eddie, and Me

Together with my birth parents in the same room. It
was a dream come true for a moment.

Foster Parents

Geoff & Elaine

Visiting My Happily Retired Foster Parents in Arizona 2015

These two, the epitome of love

Grand Canyon, South Rim, Arizona, 2015

Dinner, 2006

Christmas, 2012

Elaine and I at Cathedral Rock, Sedona, Arizona 2015

Just sitting in the middle of a desert valley, 2015

Geoff and I plotting mischief in CT, 2016

Having fun in Salem, MA October, 2017

Shenanigans in CT, 2016

On a trip to Winslow, Arizona, 2018

My Family

Our Wedding, 1991

Family Photo
July 1993

Pregnant with Ray

Family Photo
Summer 1993

Staring at my newborn son in
wonder, 1993

Still going strong 30 years
later

Happy Baby

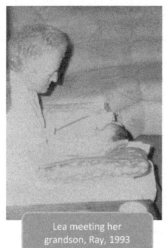

Lea meeting her grandson, Ray, 1993

Sharon, so happy to meet and hold her grandson, Ray, 1993

My mother-in-law, Barbara, in awe, holding her grandson on Mother's Day, 1993

My World, My Son
Ray, 30

David and Denise

Tom's Trio

Saying good-bye to our father

Through The Years

Baby Years

Just Born, 1969

Tom watching me

Lea tending to me

Happy Baby

Tom playing with me

Lea posing with me

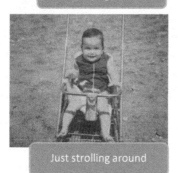
Just strolling around

No smiling

236

Toddler Years

Teen Years – Foster Care

In my bedroom in the first group home placement

Teddy Bear hugs in first group home

Group photo in second group home placement

Just a casual photo with grounds caretaker of second group home

Reunion with some of the girls from both group homes, 2010

Celebrating My Culture Through Native Powwows

High School Graduation

Senior Photo taken 1987

High School Graduation
Class of 1988

Discovering My Native Roots as a Teen

"Today I stand as a proud Mohawk Woman!" ~ *Michelle*